Letter From Washington

by

Austin Kiplinger

© 2011 Austin Kiplinger

All rights reserved. No part of this book may be reproduced or transmitted in any form or by any means, electronic or mechanical, including photocopying, recording, or by any information storage and retrieval system, without written permission of the publisher.

ISBN - 13: 978-0-578-07393-4

Printed in the United States of America
Signature Book Printing, www.sbpbooks.com

Author's Note

This didn't start out to be a book.

It began as a random collection of notes I had written over the years about people and events I had been involved with. But gradually a story seemed to be evolving, with a certain rough chronology.

It's the story of my early experiences growing up in Washington in the Twenties and Thirties, college years in the Great Depression and the ensuing career of newspaper reporter, Navy pilot, magazine editor and broadcast journalist on radio and TV. The venues were Washington, Europe, Ithaca, San Francisco, the South Pacific, Washington, Chicago and Washington again.

Those experiences spanned 38 years —less than half of my life so far. So this is "half a book." But beware! I have a pile of notes left, and sooner or later they may turn into another half book.

It is customary for authors to list the people who have been instigators or conspirators in the writing of a book. But this has always made me nervous, because I know I will leave someone out. To guard against this, I am not going to list any sources or participants. But I want to give special thanks to my assistant, Heather Riggins, who endured almost endless rounds of revision and procrastination, and to my son, Knight Kiplinger, a talented writer and editor, who helped me straighten out some kinks in my memory and some underlying facts.

So, here is a "half book." I hope you find something of interest in it.

Austin Kiplinger
Washington, D.C.
June 2011

Contents

1. The City that People Love to Hate   1
2. Every Monday Morning   9
3. Getting There: Family Origins   18
4. Life Along the Potomac   28
5. Campus Life in the '30s   49
6. You Gotta Getta a Job   62
7. Time Out for War   85
8. A New Kind of Magazine   110
9. Chicago! Chicago!   122
10. TV or Not TV   138
11. Politics and Television   154
12. Getting a Handle on Washington   168

1

The City That People Love to Hate

When people write about Washington (and people frequently do), the first question that comes to mind is: Which Washington are they writing about? Is it Washington the city? Washington the government? Is it a place, or is it a state of mind? Is it an annoyance? A savior? A villain?

It is all these things at one time or another.

Ceremonial Washington is respected and revered, even while the working part is being vilified. Americans love the monuments but carry a deep-seated suspicion of centralized power. Perhaps we can credit this to King George III and his tax policies toward the colonies, but whatever the source, it is still a strong influence in American political thought, expressing itself from time to time in the vocabulary of states' rights and grass-roots democracy. This attitude contributes to Washington's split personality—the great American paradox of tremendous power wielded by limited government, admired and reviled.

The very location of Washington as a city—its geographic site—is itself a product of the great governmental principle of compromise. When Alexander Hamilton's Federalists wanted the new government to assume the Revolutionary War debts of the states, Thomas Jefferson's Republicans demanded their price: a capital in the South. They struck a deal and located the new capital along the Potomac River between Maryland and Virginia, where it has lived in various conditions of glory and misery for more than 200 years.

In its twin role of local city and national capital, Washington suffers from an ongoing case of schizophrenia. When the budget of the District of Columbia is under consideration, the local citizens have to beg the federal government for support, making them feel like orphans.

For many years Washington was the youngest national capital in the world. In the early days, members of Congress from older cities viewed their days in Washington as an ordeal. They wrote disparaging letters home about their misery, and from their dolorous descriptions came the idea that Washington was "a city built in a swamp," even though parts of their own cities (Boston, Charleston and others) had also risen from tidal marshes.

Every government has its complaints about shortcomings of public services, but when Washington is involved, the whole world hears about it. On a Sunday morning a few years ago, the TV talk show host John McLaughlin vociferously described Washington as a city "beset by crime, corruption, budget deficits and an avalanche of calamities." The reason for his tantrum? The city hadn't plowed the snow in front of his house.

After the Sept. 11, 2001 terrorist attacks on New York and Washington, residents along Embassy Row in Washington were jolted by earth shocks that sent them to their telephones with frantic calls to police. They were answered with a cryptic message: "It's something that involves the Vice President's house, and the matter is secret." No one mentioned that they were building a bomb shelter for the Vice President. One neighbor said, "I'd like to know more, but I don't trust what I hear. This is Washington, after all."

Corrupted by Washington

Congressmen who get in trouble may be forgiven by their constituents under the rubric of "He was all right until he got down to Washington." Some loyal Chicagoans believed that Rep. Dan Rostenkowski (D-Ill.)—schooled in the politics of Chicago and Cook County—was "clean as a hound's tooth" until he went to Washington. Supporters of Rep. Wayne Hays (D-Ohio) considered him an upstanding, church-going public servant until he got to Washington and hired Elizabeth Ray as a secretary, though she admitted she didn't perform secretarial duties and didn't know how to type.

Like the Israelites of the Old Testament, Americans have the habit of placing their sins on the backs of scapegoats to send them out into the desert, and in this case, Washington is the desert: "It's all the fault of Washington."

All of this adds up to make Washington the ideal site for activist demonstrations that will appear on the 6 o'clock TV news. In any given year, the nation's capital is the venue for more demonstrations than any other American city—a ranking which other cities seem willing enough to cede. In the purest sense of the word, Washington is "synthetic"—a synthesis of qualities from the country as a whole... good, bad and in between.

In its role as a national news headquarters and a media center for journalists, Washington is, from time to time, characterized as a sinkhole of corruption. The Teapot Dome scandals of the 1920s were generated by President Harding's gang from Ohio, but Washington took the rap. President Truman's "six percenters" brought their shenanigans from Missouri, but again, their acts were "Washington indiscretions." And Richard Nixon's Watergate fiasco was carried out by Californians using political espionage that they had learned in California. The dateline, however, was "Washington."

"What does Washington think?" Washington thinks what the country thinks. It responds to currents from "back home"—the 50 states. And from this fact comes the accompanying fact that very little that is truly original starts in Washington, even though the programs bear the Washington label. In the early 1930s, Upton Sinclair began preaching his EPIC (End Poverty in California) plan out there, and it was joined by the Townsend Plan from Michigan, both proposing federal payments to retirees. The ideas were ridiculed, but in 1935 Congress passed the Social Security Act.

After the stock market crash of 1929 led to a full-blown depression, America flagellated Wall Street, but the next President, Franklin D. Roosevelt, turned to a Wall Street insider, Joseph P. Kennedy, to run the new regulatory agency, the Securities and Exchange Commission. The idea for the National Labor Relations

Board was brought to Washington from New York by Democratic Sen. Robert Wagner, and the law eventually became known as a product of Washington.

When opposing political parties lock horns in a standoff, journalists point to that old whipping boy called "gridlock." This is something everybody is supposed to be against, yet voters around the country don't always consider it a dirty word. People actually seem to *like* it, as a protection against too many laws and too much government—a protection against "Washington."

Real Washingtonians

One may wonder whether there are any people who qualify as "Washingtonians." The truth is, there are many different kinds, just as there are many Washingtons. Some Washingtonians are African-Americans whose ancestors were brought to the place as slaves, when the land was part of Maryland and Virginia. During the Civil War others came willingly, when Congress abolished slavery in Washington (in 1862—after the war began, but before slavery was abolished everywhere at the end of the war, by the Fourteenth Amendment).

Other Washingtonians are from families whose forebears owned land and buildings in the area when the city was laid out in the 1790s. Adlumia (Lummie) Hagner lived on land that was part of the farm owned by her great-great-great grandfather, John Adlum, a contemporary of George Washington. Phillips Peter is descended from a Scotsman who came to the colonies in the mid-1700s and became the first mayor of Georgetown. Charles Carroll Carter is a descendant of three colonial families whose surnames are born by two Maryland counties.

Many more Washingtonians qualify because they raised their children in the capital city, though they themselves may have come from somewhere else. Washingtonians always seem to be "from" somewhere, though they may have been in Washington most of their lives. My father, journalist W. M. Kiplinger, lived and worked in Washington from the age of 25 until he died at 76, but when asked where he was from, he would say, "Bellefontaine, Ohio."

The myth that Washington is a transient city persists even though it isn't true. It is mainly transient inbound. When an administration changes, only a thin crust of officialdom—senior political appointees—tend to leave, and some of them stick around as lobbyists. Even the *New York Times Almanac* fell into the trap of the transiency myth. In its description of the city, it said: "Washington's problems are made worse by the city's largely transient population of government workers." In point of fact, government workers—career civil servants—are among the most permanent residents of any city anywhere.

Then there's the question of when Washington finally became a "livable town." People who have come to Washington from somewhere else usually think the place "grew up" about the time they arrived. The time could have been during the Roosevelt New Deal, or World War II, or Kennedy's "Camelot," or the Reagan years, or the Clinton 1990s, or "just yesterday"—the era of Obama. To these people, Washington was a "cultural wasteland" that only attained sophistication with, variously, the restoration of Georgetown or Capitol Hill, or the opening of fine French (or Thai) restaurants, or the building of the Kennedy Center for the Performing Arts, or the arrival of Placido Domingo at the Washington Opera. Like Rodney Dangerfield, Washington "didn't get no respect." In its 125th anniversary issue, *The Washington Post* declared 1877 as "The Year Washington Became Washington." That happened to be the year *The Post* was founded.

They Never Go Away

Former senators, secretaries of the Treasury, economic advisors and others frequently continue to live in Washington long after their political tenure ends. They find jobs in law firms, think tanks and consulting businesses, helping to grease the wheels of democratic governance.

When Sen. Russell Long (D-La.), the powerful and longtime chairman of the Senate Finance Committee, retired from the Senate, he set up shop in Washington as a lawyer in partnership with his political opposite number, Republican Sen. Paul Laxalt of Nevada. When I asked him if he didn't want to return to Louisiana, he said, "Why, no. In Louisiana, everybody asks me for money. Here in Washington, they *bring* money." Rep. Wilbur Mills (D-Ark.), a legendary chairman of the House Ways and Means Committee and acknowledged expert on taxes, retired to a law office on Eye Street. Sen. Robert Dole (R-Kan.), a onetime candidate for the presidency, joined the law firm of Verner Liipfert and stayed in the capital as husband of Sen. Elizabeth Dole (R-N.C.). When I was a young reporter in Washington, I found that the first senator from Arizona, Henry Fountain Ashurst—elected when Arizona entered the Union in 1912—was still in Washington, living quietly in an apartment on Connecticut Avenue.

Occasionally there is an exception. When Rep. Carl Albert (D) retired as Speaker of the House, he returned to McAlester, Okla., never again to return to Washington. More typical, however, was Sen. Howard Baker, a Republican from Tennessee, who moved downtown and opened a law office a few blocks from the Capitol.

The undisputed, never-go-away political champion was Everett McKinley Dirksen—congressman, senator and leader of the Republican Party. After retiring from the House of Representatives, he went back to Pekin, Ill., vowing never to return. Two years later he was back—as senator from Illinois. Americans love to quote the legendary statement that is attributed to Dirksen (correctly or not): "A billion here, a billion there, and pretty soon you're talking real money."

In all the discussion about transiency in Washington, the final word belongs to Sen. Claiborne Pell (D-R.I.): "People only leave Washington by way of the box—ballot or coffin."

2

Every Monday Morning

In the mid-1920s, a growing number of American businessmen began their work week by opening an envelope from Washington with the return address: The Kiplinger Washington Agency, Albee Building, Washington, D.C. Inside they found a four-page letter starting with "Dear Sir" and ending with "Yours very truly, *W. M. Kiplinger*."

This was *The Kiplinger Washington Letter*, which had made its first appearance on September 29, 1923. For that first letter (just a single page), Kiplinger had worked late on Friday night at his typewriter, and then had walked it to a printer to be run off in time for the Saturday morning mail. It went to about 500 businessmen and bankers with an offer for a trial subscription—$5 a year at first, but soon raised to $10 and then $15.

The author, my father, was a former Associated Press reporter from Ohio who had come to Washington in 1916 and covered the U.S. Treasury during World War I for the AP, then gone to work as the Washington research and reporting office of the National Bank of Commerce in New York City. The New York bank had said to him, "We know what they *say*. Tell us what they *mean*, and what's going to happen." They did not want the official government line. They wanted hard-headed judgment on what was most likely to come of it.

Kiplinger, still in his twenties, debunked any accounts that he thought were partisan hot-air or wishful thinking. For about a year in 1919 and early 1920, Kiplinger sent his reports to the bank's New York office, working through its chief economist, Oliver Lockhart. (Lockhart had been Kiplinger's professor of economics at Ohio State University and had recommended him for the job.) Around the bank in New York, these "letters from Kiplinger" were getting quite a reputation for realism in reporting, a good basis for daily business decisions. At the same time, reporting and writing them gave Kiplinger an appreciation of the impact of Washington decisions on practical business and on the lives of ordinary people throughout the country.

Then came a business slowdown in 1920, and the National Bank of Commerce decided to discontinue the exclusive services of its Washington correspondent. Kiplinger, then 29 years old with a wife and one-year-old son (me), was urged by his wife, Irene Austin Kiplinger, to go back to their home state of Ohio. She said that her father, Judge James Austin of Toledo, would get him a good position with the Toledo *Blade* newspaper.

But Kiplinger wanted to stay in Washington and strike out on his own. He formed the Kiplinger Washington Agency with three partners, and they began to provide information for business clients on any subject at any time, for a modest fee. The National Bank of Commerce remained a client, and the new agency added others.

Kiplinger's daily journal book included entries like these:

1920

March 30-31	Garnett Babson Bros.	Watches	7hrs
29-31	Amerding	Patents	6hrs
April 5	Printers Ink	Administrative	2hrs
Sept.	Lazard Freres NYC	Banking	$35.00

1923

Sept. 14	New York Times ed. Report	$50
21	Babson Bros. Report	$35
25	Detroit TimesEdit. Mat.	$15

1926

January	Nat'l Chain Store Groc Assoc	$50
	Congdon Office, Duluth inquiry, losses resulting from investment in Imperial Russian bonds	$20
Feb. 11	Geo. R. Baily, Harrisburg, PA. inquiry airways, airports, and development of landing fields	$25

1927

Jan.	Ernst & Ernst Washington Bulletin	$416.66
	C. Adrian Bodet NYC inquiry French fran	$150
	Amer. Exchange Irving Trust Co. Dec. figures—gold, silver, merchandise	$5
Feb.	Ernst &Ernst bulletin	$568.32
	Collins Co. NYC application for shipment of machetes	$100

In addition to selling answers to special queries, Kiplinger's agency began sending all his clients an occasional bulletin (a kind of letter) with judgments on a variety of Washington topics that he thought would be useful to all of them, whatever field they were in. And some of those clients asked him to send the same bulletin to some of their business colleagues. This gave Kiplinger the idea that the weekly letter could be a regular publication, sold separately from his other services. Thus was born, in 1923, *The Kiplinger Washington Letter*.

A Different Kind of Publication

Unpretentious and businesslike in style, it was further unglamorized by being written on a typewriter and reproduced on a mimeograph machine. When his partners saw the product, they said, "You're not going to send it out like *that*, are you?" Kiplinger said "yes," and he did. Whereupon a new style of journalism and publishing was born: straight to the point, no frills, unvarnished, written the way people talked.

That first report, one page long, looked like this:

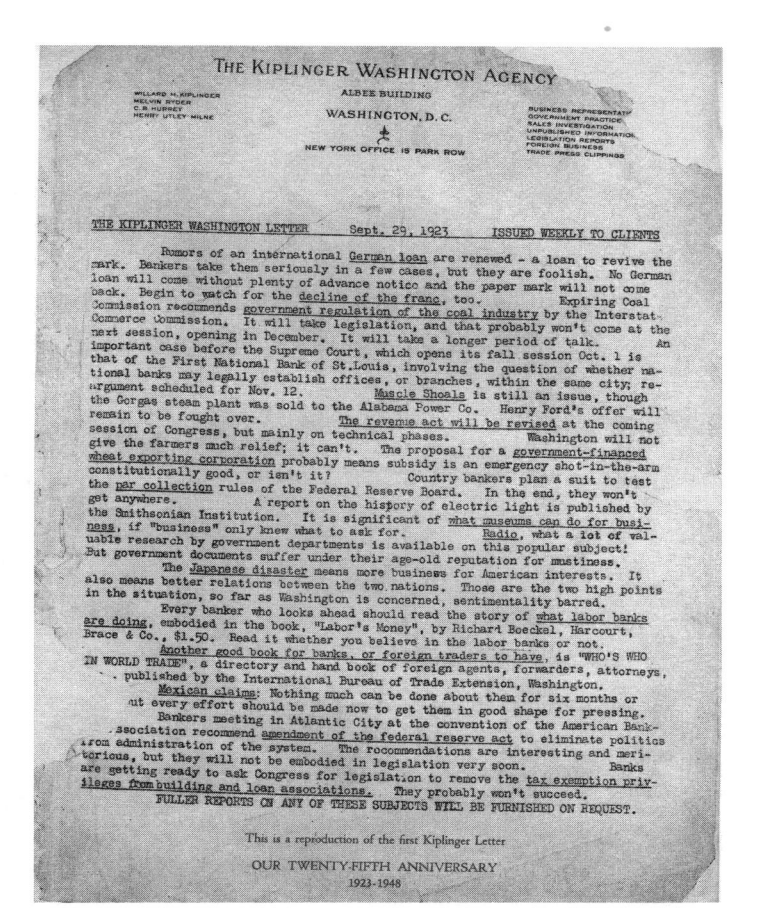

In that same year, 1923, two other young journalists, Briton Hadden and Henry Luce, began publishing *TIME, The Weekly Newsmagazine*. A year earlier, Dewitt Wallace and his wife, Lila Bell Acheson Wallace, had started clipping and pasting notable articles from American publications into a little pocket-sized magazine they called *Reader's Digest*. In 1925 a young editor named Harold Ross started putting out a magazine called *The New Yorker*. So in a four-year span, four trend-setting publications had come into existence—all of them widely imitated in the years that followed, and all of them still in publication.

Within three years of the founding of the *Letter*, all of the three partners moved on to something else. Kiplinger's first partner, Melvin Ryder, would later start *Army Times,* which subsequently grew into a large military-affairs publishing company.

The Company Expands

While Kiplinger took on an outside investor in 1925—Paul Babson of Boston—he was now largely responsible for meeting the payroll and turning out most of the copy. The staff would soon grow. The inquiry service continued. The weekly *Letter* was giving more coverage to the regulatory agencies, the Federal Reserve Board, the Interstate Commerce Commission, the Federal Trade Commission and those in the agricultural world. The Department of Commerce was becoming more active under Secretary Herbert Hoover. In 1925 Kiplinger added a biweekly *Tax Letter* to cover the Bureau of Internal Revenue.

While the American public in the Twenties perceived business as wildly prosperous, one of its largest segments—the farm economy—was in distress, having never fully recovered from the sharp drop in commodity prices after World War I. Late in the decade, President Hoover, facing a farm crisis, appointed an emergency Farm Board, and this led W. M. Kiplinger in 1929 to start the biweekly *Kiplinger Agriculture Letter*.

The subject matter was familiar to him. He had been raised in the farm state of Ohio and knew the crucial importance of the farm economy and the food industry, which then accounted for more than a third of all jobs in the U.S. A few years before, Kiplinger had cofounded, with a former agriculture professor from Ohio State, a business which offered farmers mail-order courses to help them learn marketing techniques. Kiplinger was corporate secretary of the new American Institute of Agriculture, based in Chicago, and he invested $4,000 in it. A number of other people invested $2,000 each in the new venture, among them Henry Wallace, editor of *Wallaces' Farmer* in Iowa and later Secretary of Agriculture and Vice President. When the enterprise failed, all the investors lost their money. This might not have been much for Henry Wallace, a prosperous agricultural publisher and businessman, but for W. M. Kiplinger it represented all of his life's savings.

To meet the needs of his growing editorial organization, he took on a heavy load of freelance writing for such periodicals as *Nation's Business* (later to be published by the U.S. Chamber of Commerce), *World's Work* magazine, and *The New York Times Sunday Magazine*. His most lucrative work, however, was a report on Washington developments appearing monthly in the bulletin of the Ernst and Ernst accounting firm. Through this extra editorial effort, W. M. Kiplinger kept enough income flowing into his Kiplinger Washington Agency to cover its costs, while the circulation of his Letters gradually rose through the 1920s and early '30s.

Objective Analysis

Managers of business were his readers, but Kiplinger kept close tabs on the country's political climate, which influenced legislation. Most American business people—and most of Kiplinger's readers at the time—were probably Republicans, but Kiplinger, a former

Wilsonian Democrat, was diligent in covering "the enemy"... Democrats and union labor. His contacts were extensive, and his sources welcomed an opportunity to give him their view of things, since they didn't get much objective coverage from business-oriented journalists.

To the best of my knowledge, Kiplinger was the only—or at least one of the few—reporters who found a "welcome" sign hanging at the AFL offices, or the Teamsters headquarters, or the Democratic National Committee. During those days he formed close working contacts with such political figures as Cordell Hull, the congressman from Tennessee who was then chairman of the Democratic National Committee and later Secretary of State. He also saw James Farley, who would become Postmaster General and campaign manager for Franklin D. Roosevelt.

For Kiplinger, it was important to let his readers know what they would be dealing with in organized labor and the precincts of the Democratic Party. Subsequently, during the early days of the New Deal, he was virtually the only business reporter who coolly and objectively appraised the political climate that faced business people, whether they were the manager of a corner hardware store or an executive of a major corporation. They trusted his honesty and came to believe that he would not kid them about the prospects.

When the 1929 stock market boom was heating up, Kiplinger wrote: "In quite a few conversations, the remark is that the stock market will correct itself shortly." In October, two weeks before the crash, he wrote: "Washington policy will be to dampen stock market speculation in the hope of restoring sanity." As things turned out, the market itself dampened speculation, ending in a slump which did not get back to earlier price levels until after World War II.

Friday Night at The Letter

For me, a young teenager in the early 1930s, the office of *The Kiplinger Washington Letter* was a place for hanging out on Friday nights, and a place where I could get acquainted with members of the staff. These acquaintances paid off handsomely for me as a high school student. I learned about taxes and the revenue code from John Richter. Agricultural Editor Oeveste Granducci guided me in the writing of my ambitious senior economics thesis on "The Causes and Cures of the Agricultural Problem" (at Western High School in the Georgetown section of Washington D.C., today Duke Ellington High School for the Arts).

The public scene—in America and around the world—was permeated with crises: depression, joblessness, the Japanese invasion of Manchuria, the rise of Hitler in Germany, the collapse of the League of Nations. Whatever the problems of the world, they had to be dealt with on Friday night in *The Kiplinger Washington Letter*, and they had to be translated into their practical impact. For me, the editorial discipline was beginning to form—the discipline of thinking about big events in terms of what they would mean to people at the day-to-day level of life. It was a habit I would never lose.

3

Getting There: Family Origins

Family history is like a historical novel, except that the people are real. Growing up in Washington, I often wondered what my ancestors were doing when all those famous people were running the colonies, fighting the Revolution and founding the Nation's Capital. It was natural for me to wonder about this, because every morning, as I went to high school in Georgetown, I crossed the Francis Scott Key Bridge over the Potomac River—the same river that Capt. John Smith had sailed up in 1608 on an exploratory trip from Jamestown, Va. Down the river 18 miles was George Washington's home, Mount Vernon. A few hours away were Thomas Jefferson's home, Monticello, James Madison's Montpelier, and James Monroe's homes, Ash Lawn and Oak Hill.

The fact that none of my ancestors had lived here did not mean that they were insensitive to the issues of their times. They held strong beliefs about slavery, women's rights and workers' rights, universal suffrage, prohibition, the poll tax and other matters of national concern. But they expressed their views as most people did, in their home towns around the country—at town meetings and at the polls. None of them ever considered going to Washington—until my father came along.

In 1916, Europe was at war. The Kaiser and his German forces were threatening France. The big news was coming out of London, Paris and Washington. In Columbus, Ohio, a young reporter, W. M. Kiplinger, was becoming impatient.

Born in Bellefontaine, Ohio, he had gone to Ohio State University, where he edited the student newspaper, *The Lantern,* and was one of the first two students to major in journalism. After graduating in 1912, he had written local news for Columbus' daily paper, the *Ohio State Journal,* and had worked for the Associated Press as a statehouse correspondent and editor of the state news wire. He felt it was time to move on.

His wife, Irene Austin Kiplinger, a fellow graduate of Ohio State whom he had married in 1914, wanted to go home to Toledo, where her father was Judge James Austin of the Lucas County Court. She felt that he could put in a word for her husband with his friend Grove Patterson, editor of the Toledo *Blade.*

From Ohio to D.C.

But Kiplinger had another idea. He wanted to go to Washington. Woodrow Wilson was in the White House. There was speculation that the United States might soon be involved in the war. Though it caused tension with his wife, Kiplinger quit his AP job in Columbus (where he had unsuccessfully sought a transfer to the Washington bureau), went to the capital city, and talked his way into a job with the AP Washington bureau, offering to work the night shift from 6 p.m. to 2 a.m.

He soon found himself covering the Treasury and new Federal Reserve. His senior colleagues at the White House and on Capitol Hill regarded it as a second-rate assignment, but Kiplinger found economic journalism to be very interesting. One of his sources at the Treasury was a brilliant young financier from New York, serving in the war effort as a "dollar-a-year man." His name was Eugene Meyer. Neither of these two young men could know that, one day, both of them would be publishers—Meyer of *The Washington Post*, Kiplinger of *The Kiplinger Washington Letter*—or that their soon-to-be-born children, Katharine Meyer (Graham) and Austin Kiplinger, would someday be acquainted in the civic leadership of Washington.

On Sept. 19, 1918, Kiplinger asked his boss, the AP bureau chief, for the afternoon off. He had received a call about something he needed to do. It was a quiet news day, so his request was granted, and he walked out of the AP office, down Pennsylvania Avenue, past the Capitol and up the hill to Northeast Washington. There he went into the National Homeopathic Hospital (also known as the Hahnemann Hospital) and received word that he had a son.

In that year of my birth, 1918, the city of Washington was 128 years old. The Civil War had ended only 53 years earlier. The house in which my parents lived in D.C., on Shepherd Street, N.W., was less than two miles from Fort Stevens, where Abraham Lincoln had stood on the ramparts in 1864 to watch Confederate Gen. Jubal Early's forces being beaten back from their assault on the Nation's Capital. Fifty years before that, the city had been invaded by the

British, who burned the Capitol, Navy Yard and President's House. On that occasion, Washingtonians fled. There were too few of them to put up a fight—or could it have been that they did not value their city? Just 40 miles away, thousands of Maryland volunteers rallied to drive the British from Baltimore, and Francis Scott Key wrote the words of our future national anthem, watching the bombardment of Ft. McHenry in Baltimore Harbor, while captive on a British battleship.

This all may explain why, as a young man growing up in Washington, I viewed the Nation's Capital with something of an inside-outside perspective. For me, there could be no escape from the sense of closeness to American history. The founding fathers were like a daily presence, and I tried to relate my own experiences to theirs.

German Forebears

I played a game of thinking back in time. In 1749, when my first German ancestor emigrated to America and began farming in Pennsylvania, George Washington—already a fourth-generation American—was 17 years old, learning to be a surveyor and going to work surveying the vast lands of Lord Thomas Fairfax, and signing up for the Virginia militia. That year my immigrant forebear, a German farmer named Johann Küblinger, left his home in the Palatine region of the Rhine River valley, traveled down to Rotterdam, Holland, engaged passage on an English ship to Philadelphia, and walked out to Lancaster, Pennsylvania.

My immigrant forebears owed their presence in America to an English Quaker named William Penn, who had traveled through Germany in 1677, inviting land-hungry farmers and religious dissidents to settle in his new colony of Pennsylvania. He promised them cheap land and the freedom to worship in accordance with their own consciences. This message was especially appealing to the "plain people" of the Rhine Valley, the often persecuted members of the most-conservative Protestant sects—Mennonites, Amish, Anabaptists, Brethren and Dunkards. My Küblinger and Müller (Miller) ancestors were mostly Brethren and Dunkards—so-called because they dunked their adult converts in creeks to re-baptize them. In growing numbers throughout the 18th century, these Germans answered to the dream of opportunity in a new land, even though it was then still a colony under the British king.

My Kiblinger and Miller (maternal grandmother's) forebears didn't stay long in Pennsylvania. They were probably still there in 1755, when George Washington was marching west to Fort Duquesne with British General Braddock, in the French and Indian War. But by the time of the Revolution, their offspring had traveled south to farm in the Shenandoah Valley of Virginia. Daniel Kiblinger (the English spelling of the German surname) took his family over the Allegheny Mountains by ox cart in 1806, settling in the Indian country of the Ohio Territory, near today's Springfield. His son, Phillip Kiblinger—just two when his family journeyed to Ohio—farmed in the Mad River Valley and married Mahala Shockey, who had been born in Kentucky to parents of Scottish descent from North Carolina. Phillip and Mahala Kiblinger had 12 children.

She decided she had too many in-laws of the same surname (some of whom she reportedly didn't like much), so she persuaded her husband to change the "b" to a "p," and thus the Ki*p*linger branch of the family was started.

For my family, two streams of German immigrant families—Kiplingers and Millers—came together in Bellefontaine, Ohio, in 1882, when my grandfather, Clarence Elmer Kiplinger, married my grandmother, Cora Grant Miller. Cora's grandfather was Jacob Miller, a Dunkard preacher in Ohio, who, like the Kiblingers, had journeyed west from Virginia to Ohio in the early 19th century. A later man named Jacob Miller—probably a distant cousin of my forebear—was an elder of the Dunker Church at Sharpsburg, Md., where the bloodiest fighting of the Civil War took place during the Battle of Antietam. It was a sad irony that the church of a pacifist sect would be the scene of such carnage.

My great-grandfather, Daniel Kiplinger, became a commercial builder in Lima, Ohio, where his son, my grandfather, Clarence Kiplinger, became a carpenter and then became a carriage maker. While working in the carriage company of Amos Miller in Bellefontaine, Ohio, he fell in love and married Mr. Miller's daughter Cora. They raised three sons, including my father, Willard. A few years later, the carriage business faltered, so my grandfather Clarence tried selling insurance and later took up door-to-door sales of the new Wear Ever aluminum pots and pans. In fact, he became so good at it that the whole family joined in too, making it the mainstay of the family income and putting the sons through college. In his senior years, living in the Washington area, my carpenter grandfather tried his hand at general contracting, building a few houses in Arlington, Va., one of which my grandparents, father and I lived in during the mid-1920s.

English Ancestors

Though I knew something about all this German ancestry when I was growing up, I discovered with surprise that these German ancestors had beat my English ancestors to North America by a clear 100 years. My earliest English ancestor was my great-grandfather, James Austin, who didn't set foot in America until 1849. (He arrived in America using the original family name of Aspden or maybe a variant, Asten, but later changed it to Austin.) Back home in Padiham, England, a textile and coal-mining town in Lancashire, he had been a foreman in a cotton weaving mill, until he got into trouble for his radical beliefs. A Unitarian by religion, he advocated a 10-hour work day and universal education for the children of workingmen. He was finally fired for refusing to work on Christmas. Blacklisted by the mill owners, he left England and became a mill foreman in Woonsocket, R.I. There he became an outspoken citizen and champion of labor rights at town meetings and other public gatherings.

In his new homeland he married Tammy Jane Whiting of Wrentham, Mass., whose grandfather, Elkanah Whiting, had been a farmer during the American Revolution. When George Washington issued a call for recruits in 1777, Elkanah signed up for a six-month hitch in the Massachusetts militia. While there is no record that he ever encountered a British Redcoat, his enlistment papers enabled my grandfather, Judge James Austin, Jr., to join the Sons of the American Revolution and attend their national congress in Toledo, Ohio, in 1910.

James Austin, Jr. grew up in Woonsocket, graduated Phi Beta Kappa from Brown University in 1880, taught school briefly and became a lawyer in Providence, R.I. Then he went west and worked as a lawyer, prosecutor and judge in Toledo, becoming one of the earliest juvenile court judges in the United States. (In his spare time he taught courses in Latin, Greek and law.) In Toledo James Austin, Jr. met a clerk at the courthouse named Mina ("Minnie") Weber, the daughter of a Toledo clothing store owner of German descent. During their courtship they both sang in a church choir. Their daughter, Irene—the middle child between two boys—met my father at Ohio State.

Farmers, builders, carriage makers, a lawyer and judge, a haberdasher, sellers of cookware: That was the line-up of my forebears until my father came along and became a journalist. My father used to joke that he had become a journalist because his father, a carriage maker, had become "technologically unemployed"—done in by the automobile.

But my father had, from an early age, been interested in becoming a reporter. There may also have been some influence from the life of his uncle Edward Kiplinger, who was a newspaperman in Arizona and California. Uncle Ed had acquired a reputation as a fearless foe of lawlessness. Having had consumption (tuberculosis) in his youth, he told desperadoes, "I've only got one lung and not very long to live, so go ahead and shoot." He ended up as editor of the *San Bernardino Sun* in California—and lived to be nearly 90.

Honest Men and Strong Women

These forebears of mine were practical, utilitarian. They had a common-sense approach to life: "What you believe at home, you believe at work," my grandfather Kiplinger, the carriage maker, told me. He said his father, Daniel Kiplinger, the Lima builder, had "a creed of justice and honor," based on the customer's interests as much as his own. My grandfather put this into practice in the houses he built in Arlington, Va., building more quality into them than the market expected—or would pay for. He sold a house for $3,000, but it cost him $3,500 to build. He didn't stay in the building business very long.

The women among my forebears shared a trait of strong-mindedness. When "women's lib" attracted headlines in the 1960s, I wondered what all the shouting was about. As a boy, when I visited the U.S. Capitol building, my Grandmother Kip had made sure that I went down to the lower-level crypt to see the huge marble statue depicting Elizabeth Cady Stanton, Susan B. Anthony and Lucretia Mott—leaders of the campaign for women's suffrage. We boys irreverently described the statue—three busts rising from a huge block of rough-cut marble—as "three ladies in a boat."

Not only was Grandmother Kip a staunch supporter of voting rights for women, she was also a prohibitionist, and she paid homage to this by naming her son, my father, after two prominent women prohibitionists: Frances *Willard*, national president of the Women's

Christian Temperance Union, and Henrietta *Monroe*, president of the Ohio WCTU. Embarrassed to be named after two teetotaling women, my father preferred to be called "Kip," and he mostly used his initials professionally.

Why pay all this attention to origins? If you followed the teachings of the twentieth-century French philosopher Jean-Paul Sartre, you would believe that our lives are "existential," and we live only in the moment. I'm not so sure about that. I think we live as a part of the continuity of history, and how we got to where we are is an integral part of our own life. So, to all those forebears—the earlier Küblingers, Kiplingers, Millers, Austins, Shockeys and Webers—I tip my hat and bow in appreciation of their energy, enterprise and independence.

4

Life Along the Potomac

When I was a boy, New York had its Larchmont and Bronxville. Chicago had its Oak Park, Lake Forest and Winnetka. Proper Bostonians might live in Brookline or Cambridge. But Washington had no real counterpart, except maybe Chevy Chase, Md. For years, people who lived in the suburban outskirts of Washington thought of themselves as Marylanders or Virginians. The historic town of Alexandria, which looks across the river at Washington, was part of the Old Dominion, even though it had been part of the District of Columbia until given back to Virginia in 1846.

After World War I, a trickle of government workers, congressional aides and assorted professionals began taking up residence across the Potomac River in Virginia, in places like Arlington, Alexandria and Falls Church. I had been born in the District of Columbia and lived there in early childhood, but eventually I moved across the river too.

When I was born, I had been taken home from the Hahnemann Hospital in 1918 to a little row house on Shepherd Street off Georgia Avenue in Northwest Washington, in an area known as Petworth.

When I could barely walk, the family moved a few blocks away to Grant Circle, named for Civil War General and later President Ulysses S. Grant. Then came a Victorian row house in the 1100 block of Harvard Street, in a quiet, older neighborhood known as Columbia Heights.

My parents' marriage had been strained for some time. My mother had a longing for her hometown of Toledo, Ohio, and my father was focused on establishing his new editorial firm in Washington. They separated when I was four. My mother and my two-year-old sister, Jane Ann, went back to Toledo, and I stayed in Washington with my father and my Kiplinger grandparents. My parents divorced a few years later.

My father and his father—my grandfather—had talked about building a house together...the journalist and the former carpenter/carriage maker. By 1924 the post-World War I real estate boom was cooling, and some developers were going broke. In the Virginia suburb of Arlington, a real estate operator named Ruby Lee Minor was having trouble with her development called Lee Heights, so building lots were for sale at bargain prices. My father bought one on a little street called Spring Drive, named for a spring where President Theodore Roosevelt had watered his horse when he was out riding with his physician, Adm. Presley Marion Rixey. The street was only paved with gravel and had only three or four houses on it—a perfect setting for another house. The two Kiplingers proceeded to build one, with my grandfather supervising construction, and in 1924 we moved into it—my father, grandparents Clarence and Cora Kiplinger and six-year-old Austin.

29

Life in Arlington

The new and ragged Lee Heights was a prototypical version of the failed real estate dream of the middle 1920s. At one end was an unfinished, partially sculpted street curving up into the woods, with one Spanish-style house sitting defiantly on the top of the hill, with a driveway leading up from the dirt street. At the other end was a dusty, semi-finished tennis court—a lonely vestige of the developer's promise of "modern amenities." An inter-urban electric trolley—the Old Dominion Railway—ran alongside it. We used the tennis court for sandlot football scrimmages.

Among the venturesome neighbors—government employees, biologists, Foreign Service officers, journalists and trade association staffers—one source of excitement was "ooh-ing and ah-ing" over every new automobile that anyone brought home, whether it was a Graham-Paige, an Essex, a Star, a Willys Overland or a Nash—all leading brands of their time. My father had just sold his old Lexington, the one he had learned to drive in. Learning to drive at that time consisted of a brief instruction by the salesman, followed by a do-it-yourself tryout, and then driving the car home—in my father's case, going around and around Grant Circle until he figured out how to stop it. But now we were in the suburbs, and whoever had a car found himself offering to take someone out for a drive. The automobile was still a major source of excitement.

A close second on the excitement scale was the radio. We had a radio set at home—a crystal set. The 1924 Democratic National Convention in New York City was the first convention to be broadcast by radio, and it held special significance for me, because my father was covering it. It turned out to be longest nominating struggle on record (103 ballots), during which the Alabama delegates repeatedly cast "24 votes for Oscar W. Underwood," its favorite-son senator. (Ultimately the delegates nominated John W. Davis, who was defeated by incumbent President Calvin Coolidge.)

For me, the crystal set was magic. It was a little box with a piece of crystalline galena or fool's gold in the bottom and a spindly wire at the end of a stylus. With the aid of earphones, I could actually detect sounds transmitted through the air from a radio station 25 miles away. Say what you will about space travel, the experience of a crystal set radio was about as breathtaking as anyone could imagine (unless you had read Jules Verne's *Twenty Thousand Leagues Under the Sea*). In the midst of the convention proceedings (broadcast from New York to a station in D.C.), I took the tiny stylus and scratched the little wire back and forth across the crystal, listening, and listening, and listening—and finally, there it was! A human voice, croaky and scratchy, but identifiably a human voice!

A couple of years later, with my friend Robert Richardson, I rigged up a tin can telegraph system, stretching a wire across the street from his house to mine. The sounds we got were mostly screeches.

Inventions of the Twentieth Century came tumbling out, one after the other: the airplane, the radio, newer automobiles, the electric refrigerator, the safety razor with a disposable blade. To me, however, one of the most appreciated was...the Iron Fireman! Yes, ladies and gentlemen, the Iron Fireman—a wondrous machine that automatically stoked your home furnace with coal, a task previously performed by the man of the house or his children. The hopper held coal. You filled it in the morning and it lasted all day. An Archimedes screw slowly fed the coal into the bottom of the fire box, where it burned and warmed the house. Then in the evening, you shook the grate to get the ashes out of the fire box into the lower level, from where you could shovel them out. When the ash can was filled, you emptied it into the street, filling the ruts with ashes and hoping they would pack down solidly before the next rain. Only in America!

Downtown

Though our neighborhood of Arlington, Va., was called Cherrydale, our mail address was Rosslyn—a rundown collection of pawnshops, second-hand furniture stores and an old brewery. Relatives would come from Ohio to look us up. They would go to Rosslyn, look around, shake their heads and think, "Poor Kip, he must have fallen on hard times."

Rosslyn was just across the Potomac River from Georgetown, which for many years had been the southern terminus of the Chesapeake & Ohio Canal. Boats had floated across the river in a sluiceway on the lower level of an historic stone aqueduct, with vehicular traffic on a roadway above. A major engineering wonder when it was completed in the 1840s, the Aqueduct Bridge was now a derelict. In 1923 it was replaced by the new, concrete Francis Scott Key Bridge, dedicated by President Calvin Coolidge.

For me the new bridge was the pathway to the city. On Saturdays I used it to visit the Mall and the Smithsonian museums. There

I found an endless feast of wonders— American Indian artifacts, prehistoric fossils, early airplanes and automobiles. I was visiting the Smithsonian one day with my grandfather Kiplinger when, to my astonishment, he (the former carriage maker) pointed to one of the little black machines and said, "I helped make that." I asked, "How can you know that? They all look alike." Pointing to the body of the horseless carriage, he said, "I had a special way of turning a molding, and I think you'll find it on this body." Then he told me to go around back and look. Sure enough, there it was! I recall that the car was an 1894 Haynes, from Kokomo, Ind., considered the first commercially viable automobile made in America. My grandfather told me that he had worked in the Haynes factory in 1894. When I was older, I learned from my father that his father's small carriage shop in Bellefontaine, Ohio had failed in the Panic of 1893, so Grandfather Kiplinger ended up working in Indiana for a while. When I last visited the National Museum of American History, in recent years, that Haynes automobile was still there.

The Mall in those days provided a space where boys from Virginia could arrange a pick-up game of football with kids from Southeast Washington, who were, as we said then, "colored." They were tougher than we were and usually won, but we played together and no one got hurt. The schools were segregated in Washington, Maryland and Virginia back then, and not until years later, when I went to college at Cornell and Harvard, did I meet some of the "other Washingtonians" who had gone to school when I did but in schools that were designated by race.

Showing the Town

The annual White House Easter Egg Roll, held on Easter Monday, attracted many families from around the country. For me and my entrepreneurial buddy, Woody Saugstad, these out-of-town visitors were "pigeons." They were not permitted to go onto the South Lawn of the White House unless accompanied by a child, and we were willing and able to be that child, escorting them for 25 cents a trip. We couldn't do more than two trips a day, but a 50-cent day more than paid for carfare.

Later I became a tour guide for visiting relatives from Ohio, and I developed a kind of sightseeing patter. Across the street from the White House stands a heroic monument of the Marquis de Lafayette, the young French nobleman who helped the American colonies fight the War of Independence. He has a robe draped over his arm, and at his feet is a bare-breasted woman with her arm outstretched, offering him a sword. With the authority of a sightseeing guide, I would tell my visitors that she was saying, "Give me back my coat, and you can have your damned old sword!"

Another venue for the visitors was the junction of Connecticut Avenue, Columbia Road and California Street. Here stands a statue of Gen. George McClellan, commander of the Union army in the Civil War, who was noted for his indecision and reticence to fight, leading to his demotion by Lincoln. The location of the monument at the junction of so many streets, I explained, gave General McClellan "six avenues of retreat." In front of the National Archives, on the Pennsylvania Avenue side, I would point out two huge statues. On the base of one is inscribed, "What is Past is Prologue." I explained to my tourists that this is government jargon for "You ain't seen nothin' yet."

On Sunday mornings, I would ride with my father to Georgetown to pick up a copy of the *New York Times*, for which he wrote freelance articles. After the stock market crash in 1929, followed by deepening depression in the early Thirties, he was increasingly in demand as an analyst of economic policy, and he frequently wrote on such Hoover economic recovery plans as the Federal Farm Board, public works programs and the Reconstruction Finance Corporation. The "newsstand" was at the Georgetown end of Key Bridge, in the form of a lone newsboy who sold us a full Sunday paper with extra sections for 10 cents. As I hauled in the paper, my father would ask, "Did we make this week?" (newspaper slang for "Did we *make the paper*...is my article there?"). I would tell him yes or no. It mattered greatly, because every freelance payment would help pay the rent at the office.

The first Kiplinger office was on 15th Street across from the U.S. Treasury, in the Albee Building, which also housed Keith's Theater, a leading stop on the national vaudeville circuit. My father's second-floor office was behind the theater marquee, which reduced the rent. (Upstairs were the first quarters of the National Press Club.) I could climb out the window and sit on the marquee to watch parades turn the corner at 15th and Pennsylvania and come right past below me, including the one for Calvin Coolidge's inauguration on March 4, 1925, when I was six years old. From there I saw World War I tanks rumbling up the street, clanking on the steel rails of the streetcar tracks.

It was at about this time that I started to collect wooden match boxes—an arcane hobby. Some were made in the United States by the Ohio Match Company, and others were made in Sweden by companies controlled by Ivar Krueger, one of the richest men in the world. Mr. Krueger, I learned, also collected matchboxes; his motive was to keep track of his competition. Through my father's tax editor, John Richter, I established contact with Mr. Krueger, who asked me if I would like to sell him my collection. I asked an exorbitant price of 10 cents a box ($12.70 for 127 boxes), and I thought I had pulled a smart one on the Match King. I later suspected that Richter actually bought my collection himself and didn't send it to Krueger. (Krueger's global empire collapsed in the Great Depression, and he killed himself in 1932.)

To Fly

The Twenties were heady days for boys in America. In May, 1927, Charles Lindbergh flew solo across the Atlantic. Aviation was only 24 years old, and it still carried the unknowns of experimentation, risk and records to be set. I was consumed with excitement about it. Lucky Lindy was constantly in my thoughts, and I virtually memorized his best-selling account of the flight, *We*. Even now, I can remember that the dimensions of his plane, the "Spirit of St. Louis," were a 46-foot wingspan and 28-foot fuselage. Our wooden models of the plane were crude, but I had my picture taken, proudly holding mine. Our miniature flying machines were balsa wood contraptions called Baby ROGs ("rise off the ground") that would stay in the air and fly perhaps 50 yards—far shorter than the distance covered by the original Wright Brothers' flying machine in 1903 at Kitty Hawk.

Two years later, I followed the exploits of Adm. Richard E. Byrd on his flight over the South Pole. Some time thereafter—to my almost unbelievable good fortune—I flew with Adm. Byrd's co-pilot, Bernt Balchen. Though aviation was glamorous, jobs were scarce for pilots. They had to make their living as best they could—some by offering sightseeing flights over Washington, using the Hoover Airport, a muddy collection of landing strips and hangars at the south end of the 14th Street Bridge, where the Pentagon now stands.

On a Saturday morning, my father and I climbed into in a high-wing monoplane with an open back-seat cockpit cut all the way down to the floor. Pilot Balchen took off, banked over the monuments, the White House, and the Capitol, flew up and down the river, and then shouted that we were going back to land. Back on the ground, with the engine cut and propeller stopped, he climbed out of his cockpit, slid back on the wing and said to us, "OK, you can unbuckle your belt now." *Unbuckle my belt?* I hadn't buckled anything! I didn't know anything about seat belts, but Balchen was a good pilot, and his turns were smooth and well banked, so I didn't fall out.

Near our house in Virginia lived Lt. Cdr. Bastedo, a naval aviator. On his return from cross-country flights, he would buzz his house to tell his wife he would soon be home to dinner. Though I couldn't articulate it then, I suspect a seed was planted: flying was something I might want to do someday.

The thought of passengers traveling by air, as we would travel on trains, never entered my mind until one day my father asked if I would like to take a trip in an airplane from Washington to Baltimore.

All the way to Baltimore? Wow! We would sit in plush seats, beside an aisle, just like being at home. So we took off from the Hoover Airport in a big two-wing craft with wires and struts that made it look like a disjointed turkey buzzard.

It was Curtiss Condor, named for the bird that soars like an eagle. Whether it was a soaring condor or an ugly ducking, it took us to Baltimore, and for me the age of commercial aviation had begun.

Games We Played

I remember seeing dramatic silent movies about the World War that had ended just a few years before, like *The Big Parade* in 1925 (with John Gilbert) and *Wings* in 1927, starring Buddy Rogers and Clara Bow. For me, however, the most tangible reminder of the Great War was an elegant German officer's helmet that my father had bought after the war. (My father had tried to enlist in the Army during the war, but was apparently rejected for flat feet.) When we played war, I would wear the helmet and play the role of "Hun." My side always lost.

There were no intramural sports—or sports of any kind—at my elementary school, so we made do with a boxing club in a converted chicken coop behind Bob Thomas' house on Lorcom Lane. Football scrimmages were in the field across the street. For "track events," we dug a pit for pole vaulting and put into service some bamboo poles that had been center rods for rugs. In high school I decided to become to discus thrower, but my coach had no interest in discus throwing, so I bought my own discus. I got it at the Vim Sporting Goods store on downtown G Street. I also had to buy a book to learn how to throw it. I never became an accomplished discus thrower, but I did win the bronze medal in a college intramural contest.

Football was, even then, a hot topic. We paid attention to who won the Big Ten, the Ivy League and the Rose Bowl. When USC won the Rose Bowl in 1933, their star quarterback, Irvine "Cotton" Warburton, ran rings around the defense (exciting stuff). Easterners sang an irreverent version of the USC fight song: "Time out for USC, the captain wants his salareee! The halfback's in a rage, he didn't get his weekly wage—and subsideee!"

Mechanical devices for the sporting world were not here yet. Tennis rackets were big and heavy (and mine had a wide wooden frame). Skateboarding was on whatever you could make with a board and a pair of skates. Skiing wasn't big around Washington. Our mid-Atlantic weather did not include much snow. When a little ice formed on the Reflecting Pool by the Lincoln Memorial, only our friends from Minnesota would skate.

But there was always "Cowboys and Indians." Along the valleys of Donaldson Run and other tributaries to the Potomac, I found Indian arrowheads and skin scrapers— stones with one side sharpened for scraping the flesh off wild animal skins. I kept my valuables in a wooden box under my bed. In a second box, I kept Civil War relics: Minie balls that came out of Leissler's barn on Lee Highway, left 60 years earlier by Union soldiers on their way to the Battle of Bull Run. And buckles and water canteens, all from Union troops. Though Arlington was part of Virginia and the Confederacy, the heights around Washington had been commandeered by the federal government, and the city was ringed with Union forts to protect the capital. So 60 years later, these forts were the playground for boys reenacting skirmishes.

When my father wanted to give us boys a treat, he would see to it that we got tickets to pro wrestling matches with the two biggest stars, Gus Sonnenberg and his trademark "Flying Tackle" against Jim Londos, "The Golden Greek." They were both world champions, but I recall Londos usually winning.

Books We Read

When I was about ten years old, Grandfather Kiplinger gave me a copy of Hendrik Willem van Loon's *Story of Mankind*, a panoramic view of the sweep of human civilization, so I got an early interest in history. My favorite books were stories of life out of doors, like *Rolf in the Woods* by Ernest Thompson Seton, about the Indian Quonab who lived under a rock in western Connecticut with his dog Skookum. (Rolf was a young scout for the Americans during the Revolutionary War.)

My father would bring me books that his friends had written and inscribed: *The Origins of Tennis*, in elegant hand-bound leather; *Our Times,* by the journalist Mark Sullivan; and the enchanting books of A.A. Milne, *When We Were Very Young* and *Winnie-the-Pooh.* (I still vividly remember such favorite poems as "James James, Morrison, Morrison, Weatherby George Dupree" and "Jonathan Jo has a mouth like an O and a wheelbarrow full of surprises.")

I think van Loon's *Story of Mankind* won the day. I still remember his account of climbing to the top of the tower in Rotterdam, peering out over the city, and thinking about how that city had come up from the tidal sands of the North Sea. (My hometown, too—Washington—had come out of tidal marshes.) Van Loon's ideas seemed to contradict what I later heard in classes at school, but they taught me that the way people live does not always conform to the descriptions that historians write.

Other books I enjoyed as a boy and teenager included *Treasure Island, Robinson Crusoe,* Carl Carmer's *Listen for a Lonesome Drum,* and *The Secret Garden,* by Washington author Frances Hodgson Burnett.

My booklist was not as long as the 24-page list of books that historian Arthur Schlesinger, Jr. later said he had read in childhood, but Schlesinger (the son of a college friend of my father's) was a child prodigy. For me, boyhood reading was just a spontaneous pastime which, in retrospect, I still cherish.

Shows We Saw

Of all stereotypes of the Twenties, probably the most universal is "the movies," because it was in that decade that motion pictures, mostly silent, became mass entertainment. Few people who grew up after the First World War were far from a moving picture theatre. However strict the family was, there was nearly always a movie that would pass muster after a careful perusal of *Parents' Magazine.* When others failed to make the grade, by the early Thirties there was always one starring Shirley Temple. For my buddies and me, the standard fare was westerns—Hoot Gibson, Tom Mix and all the rest. For 10 cents, you could see a string of westerns at 9th Street movie houses, and if you wanted to, you could stay all day. Though I had heard of "nickelodeons," we didn't have any in Washington; for us the cheapest rate was 10 cents. Regular movies—non-westerns—cost more, 25 and 30 cents. For 60 cents at the Fox Theater in the National Press Building—where my father's staff moved in as inaugural tenants in 1927—you could see a movie plus parts of a live stage show from New York.

For comedies there were Laurel and Hardy and Charlie Chaplin. Even now, if I am confronted by a tough piece of steak, I think of Charlie Chaplin in *The Gold Rush*, where he boils his shoes and gently plucks the nails from between his teeth. In *The Black Pirate*, Douglas Fairbanks, Sr. plunged his knife into the cloth of a tall sail and rode the long jagged slit to the deck of the ship.

Keith's Vaudeville Theatre brought Chinese jugglers and sold chocolate candy bars from a 5-cent dispenser on the back of the seat (but not popcorn). Blackstone the Magician appeared at Poli's Theatre on Pennsylvania Avenue, at a site where—110 years earlier—British General Ross and Admiral Cockburn had eaten their meal and drunk ale while watching their fire burn the White House.

In 1926 my father married a British writer named Leslie Jackson, so I now had a stepmother—but not for long. They had a son, Peter, in 1928 and were divorced in '31. Leslie loved the theater (and even did some playwriting herself), and she introduced me to "legitimate theater" at the Belasco, on Lafayette Square across from the White House. Peter Pan would fly across the stage and disappear into the curtains behind the wings. There, too, my stepmother introduced me to the witty plays of Noel Coward, and I decided that actors on the stage all spoke with a British accent.

While I never had any ambition to play dramatic parts, school exacted performances from everyone, so, in seventh grade, I strode across the stage in the Thanksgiving pageant, portraying a turkey, and proclaiming:

I am master of all I survey,
My right there is none to dispute.
Let the Gods send what trials they may,
I will meet them and beat them to boot."

(Applause; retire to the right.)

In a local version of Major Bowe's Original Amateur Hour, the hit national radio program of the 1930s, Alexandria radio station WJSV had a Saturday morning talent show, and the Washington-Lee Junior High School Special Kazoo Band, of which I was a member, played on the program. (Elder Solomon Lightfoot Michaux, our leading black evangelist in Washington, proclaimed in his radio ministry on WJSV that the station's call letters stood for "*W*illingly *J*esus *S*uffered for *V*ictory," but they actually were the owner's initials.)

Music We Heard

There were two major sources of music for the average American home in the 1920s: the phonograph and the radio. Our phonograph was an RCA Victor, and the music ranged from Irish tenor John McCormack to the operatic arias of Enrico Caruso and Amelita Galli-Curci. "The Voice of Firestone" came over the radio on Sunday afternoons, sponsored by the tire company. On Monday nights there was Harry Horlick and his A&P Gypsies, sponsored by the grocery chain.

When serious orchestral music was the order of the day, we attended concerts of the National Symphony Orchestra, which had been formed in 1931 under conductor Hans Kindler. With my piano teacher, Lucille Saugstad, I heard the National Symphony in Constitution Hall, sitting high above the stage and following the music with an orchestral score. My introduction to symphonic music had been at the first children's concerts of the National Symphony Orchestra on Saturday mornings in the auditorium of Central High School.

Joys and Sorrows of the River

It is not a coincidence that most of the great capitals of the world are located on rivers. When these cities were growing, rivers were the principal avenues of commerce and the highways of history. They came to be spoken of in reverent terms. The Thames, the Seine, the Tiber, and even the Moscow featured in heroic sagas.

In the days of European discovery, the Potomac River was considered a desirable waterway. But when the fledging city of Washington began to emerge in the early 1800s, the capital's detractors began to describe the river in derogatory terms. Later in the twentieth century, writers used its name to deprecate a rival, accusing him of catching "Potomac fever."

All this notwithstanding, in my earlier memories, the Potomac River was friendly. When I was about three years old, father took me to the Washington Canoe Club, where he kept his Old Town canoe, sat me between the gunwales and paddled gently out across the water while I—according to my father's account—beamed joyfully. My mother, however, was protesting violently on shore. She regarded the whole operation as a dangerous escapade, and the argument apparently escalated to such a degree that it may have contributed to my parents' subsequent separation.

None of this, however, dampened my childish spirits, and my memory now recalls the day as a huge success and the river as a friendly venue. In years to come, our Old Town canoe, painted dark red, continued to be a source of pleasure for my father and me until it was washed away from Sycamore Island in the Great Flood of 1936—the worst flood in the mid-Atlantic region since the Johnstown (Pa.) Flood of 1889.

In the 1930s, my father bought a 30-acre wooded tract on the Virginia side of the river below Great Falls. It was near Black Pond, which subsequently became a part of the campus of The Madeira School for girls. On my father's land were a rustic cabin and an earthen dam holding back just enough water for a dip on sweltering days. The river nearby was treacherous, so we usually left it alone, but on one Thanksgiving, before we were due back home for the ceremonial dinner, the weather was unseasonably warm, and my father and I decided to go for a swim in the Potomac. At a sandy cove, we stripped and plunged in. Just as fast, we plunged out. The water, which had tumbled over the Great Falls of the Potomac, was icy cold. After less than a minute, we decided we had made our point. Clothed again and back home, we were able to say that we had been swimming in the Potomac on Thanksgiving.

In springtime, the banks of the river were verdant. Tributary streams flowed through misty valleys of laurel and wild azaleas. These were woods in which the Analostan Indians, the Piscataway, and the wandering Susquehannas had hunted 300 years earlier. We watched the trailing arbutus send out its little sentinels of spring. Then came the red buds of the Judas Tree, followed by the white dogwood blossoms. Before these, the shadbush would dot the gray woods with their white flowers announcing spring.

This was the time when shad would be running upstream in the river. My father's friend Felix Saugstad was the guru of the shad bake. With great ceremony and preparation, the neighborhood men would convene on Saturday to prepare for their Annual Shad Bake. In the evening, beside an open fire, the fish would be split open, spread out, and tacked onto wooden boards propped up to take the heat from the smoldering fire. In Prohibition days, no one spoke about whiskey, but as the evening wore on, there was more joviality among the men. When the coals were glowing, the shad would be slathered with a concoction of butter, salt and pepper. When the shad was served, the joy was indescribable. *Gourmet* magazine would have a hard time recreating the scene of a Potomac River shad bake.

The River's Dark Side

During the summer before my tenth birthday, with my friend Robert Richardson, I was invited to visit my Uncle Gale and Aunt Jeannette Kiplinger in Buffalo, New York. The thought of riding a train overnight, going to bed in a sleeping car and waking up in New York was irresistible, and the appeal was further heightened by the prospect of seeing Niagara Falls.

But before we left, Robert and I had to finish a project that we were pursuing—to build and test some self-propelled wooden boats.

We had already made a tin-can telegraph system between our houses. Now, in preparation for the boat project, we cut two one-foot-by-six-inch boards, pointed them at the front ends and notched them at the other. We rigged them with heavy-duty rubber strips twisted tightly around flat wooden propellers. In the water, the resistance would allow the propeller to rotate evenly and push the boat ahead. That was the theory, but it had to be tested in the water, and the nearest water was the Potomac River, a mile and half down Donaldson Run from our homes.

On a warm Saturday morning, we took our boats under our arms and walked down the creek to the river's edge. Since I had not yet learned to swim, it was up to Robert to dog-paddle behind the boats using a flotation cushion in front of him. Robert stripped down to his skivvies and waded in. His boat would be first. We wound it up, put it in the water and off it went, with Robert paddling along behind.

As the boat picked up speed we were elated, and Robert paddled faster. The current was by now pushing the cushion farther ahead and he was thrashing hard to keep up. Suddenly he realized it was outdistancing him, and he became frantic. Despite his best efforts, he couldn't reach it for support. He called out for help. Upstream, some older boys heard his call and ran down to where I stood on the shore, and one of them plunged in. Robert's cries became more desperate. He began to sink and reappear. Then he went under and didn't reappear. There was no more sound. I was dumbstruck helpless. Robert was nowhere to be seen. The older boy was still some distance away. I screamed, but there was nothing anyone could do. The older boy came back to shore. We all looked at each other. They said they were sorry, and then they left. Robert was gone. I was alone.

I picked up my boat and started walking up the trail that we had come down half an hour before—past Military Road, past the pond, past the Spanish House and the spring house, past my piano teacher's house and back to where Robert lived. What would I say to his mother and his uncle and aunt? What would I do? I knocked on the door. Mr. MacDonald came, opened the screen door, and I blurted out, "Robert drowned. Robert drowned at the river." I heard a scream, and I walked home.

But the woods were my friend…and the stream, with its trailing arbutus and frogs, and the banks that were covered with laurel and wild azaleas. It was there that I could be sad without showing it—or happy in the change of seasons, not far from home but alone when it was good to be alone. Not many people have the sanctuary of the woods, as our lives get crowded together. It's too bad.

5

Campus Life in the '30s

The student demonstrations of the 1960s received more public attention (through the medium of nightly TV) and were far more violent than the political activism of my college years in the 1930s. But, while the issues of the Sixties (civil rights and Vietnam) were certainly important, the campus debates of the Thirties focused on matters of life and death for millions of people and entire nations... the Great Depression, the rise of totalitarianism and, ultimately, the second world war in just 20 years.

Across the United States during the Great Depression, classrooms, lecture halls, churches and schools were sites for debates on theology, race relations, socialism, unionization, anti-Semitism and government reforms of every description. Dictatorship, democracy and the "welfare state" were the subjects of political campaigns, and they were debated at breakfast tables as well as on campuses throughout the nation.

In the 1930s the overwhelming global problem was economic depression and massive unemployment. Dictators were capitalizing on it. Benito Mussolini proclaimed his industrial Fascism as a remedy. Adolph Hitler's Nazis proclaimed National Socialism as the answer. In Russia, where the Communist state owned everything, Joseph Stalin ruled with an iron fist, and—largely unbeknownst to the West at that time—was transporting millions of dissidents to Siberia to work and die in labor camps.

In the United States, all the tensions and political movements of the world were refracted through the American experience. They were here, but in different forms, equivalent but always with a distinct American flavor. Totalitarianism could not put down roots in America as it had in the Old World of Europe.

A Trip to Europe

My first personal experience with the rising political strife in Europe came when I was 14 years old, on a trip there with my father in September, 1932. As we landed in Hamburg after six days at sea, my father and I stood at the ship's rail watching the stevedores tie up. My father, the reporter and editor, had been writing on the Hitler phenomenon. He knew about the Nazi goose-stepping and the famous "Heil, Hitler!" salute. As our ship tied up, he jokingly raised his right arm in the familiar gesture. From behind him, a ship steward rushed up, frantically shaking his head and saying, "No, no, no! You might start a riot!"

The political mood in Germany was so tense, with Hitler threatening control, that the slightest spark might ignite a political explosion. The old and revered Field Marshal Paul von Hindenburg was still president and chancellor of Germany, but early in the following year, Hitler would usurp his power and be named chancellor. Within a few months of my father and my visit to Berlin, the capital city would be reeling from the Reichstag Fire and its frightening aftermath. (The fire was found to have been started by a deranged Dutch Communist, but he was encouraged and assisted by the Nazis, who had already made a plan to use arson as a pretense for rounding up every leftist in Germany.)

Despite the tension in Germany that fall, we were welcomed at the customary tourist venues. We strolled Unter den Linden boulevard and had dinner at the Haus Vaterland, a popular Berlin restaurant. In Paris, the atmosphere was less tense, more traditionally Parisian. We ate at the Café de la Paix, only a block from our hotel at La Place de L'Opera. My father told me that if we sat at the sidewalk café, within twenty minutes we would see someone we knew. I scoffed at the idea, but sure enough, we did. And the next day, my father helped me celebrate my 14th birthday by arranging for my first barber shave. As an additional birthday gift, my father took me to see the risqué dance hall show at the Folies Bergere on Montmartre, the Paris hill topped by L'Eglise Sacre Coeur. As we were walking home, we were accosted by one of the famous Parisian ladies of the street. She kept speaking to us in French, and my father kept shaking his head. I asked what she was saying, and he told me she wanted us to go home with her. I asked my father, "What did you say?" He said, "I told her you were too young. But she kept shaking her head and saying, *'Non, monsieur, il n'est pas trop jeune'*." So the only presents I got for my birthday were the shave and a show with dancing girls.

Debate on Campus

Three years later, in the fall of 1935, when I was a student in college, I was caught up in the great debates of our time. College students in the Thirties were looking for answers to the world's economic challenges. And so, on campuses from coast to coast, we debated the issues with extravagant rhetoric and emphatic labels, while in other parts of the world these issues were leading to war.

It was a yeasty time for young intellectuals on campus. In political philosophy, Adam Smith's *Wealth of Nations* and Jeremy Bentham's utilitarianism competed with Marx and Lenin and their Communism for the hearts and minds of students. Though we studied John Locke's treatises on liberty and freedom in political science class at Cornell, the morning newspaper accounts of President Roosevelt's Supreme Court "packing" plan were the grist for our classroom discussion. A coterie of bright young idealists got caught up in the swirl of radicalism, and some—like Alger Hiss—became guilty of deception and treason.

On American campuses, students ran in different crowds and social sets, as they always do. For me at Cornell, life was a mixture of all of them. I had roommates from various backgrounds and political persuasions, hailing from Minnesota, Ohio, New York and Peking, China. At the Telluride House—an intellectual association at Cornell—there was an itinerant Irish poet, a resident American economist, and a visiting British scholar.

My Telluride friend Teh-chang Koo ("T.C." to his buddies) was a son of the great Chinese diplomat Wellington Koo. He later returned to China to help build an aircraft industry for the Nationalist government of Chiang Kai-shek, but he found his efforts thwarted by the Japanese and the mounting Communist insurgency of Mao Tse-tung. My Telluride colleague Charles Collingwood and I were both nominated, in our senior year, to be Rhodes Scholars. I made it only to the semifinal round, but Charlie won the big prize and headed to Oxford in 1940. From there he launched his distinguished career in broadcast journalism as one of Edward R. Murrow's bright young men at CBS radio, covering the war from London and North Africa.

College Life

Some students joined fraternities and sororities, but most lived in dormitories and rooming houses and worked at part-time jobs. In those depression years, the years of the 1930s, matters of economy were facts of daily life. Scholarships were available for top high school students, but my father—whose publishing business was beginning to thrive—told me he could afford to pay the tuition and I should not take a scholarship away from someone who needed it. Though I had received the Civitan Medal for Citizenship in high school and had been voted "most likely to succeed," my father still said, "no scholarship."

I could afford to join a fraternity (Delta Upsilon and later Telluride), have my own car (a 1931 Model A Ford), and pay my bills on time. The total cost for my freshman year was about $1,250--$800 for tuition and $450 for all the rest. It sounds like very little today, but at the time I started college—1935—it was about what the average American household earned in a whole year. (That would be like a $50,000-a-year household today facing $50,000 of annual college expenses.)

When I went to Cornell, in upper New York State, the city of Ithaca still had a railroad running through it. The Lehigh Valley could deliver you from Washington on an overnight trip through Wayne Junction, Pa., but it was faster to drive (even at an average speed of 30 miles an hour), so I elected to get there in my car.

Cornell, which had been founded by a Quaker with a non-denominational and co-educational admissions policy, was a member of the Ivy League, but it stuck out like a sore thumb in that patrician group, because it had a college of agriculture (*farmers in the Ivy League!*) and a college of veterinary medicine (*a cow college in the Ivy League? Shocking!*). Furthermore, it admitted women—as no other Ivy did–and even had black students (not many, but probably more than the other Ivies in that era).

Choosing Cornell

So how did I end up there? My father and mother had graduated from Ohio State, as did one uncle (the other having gone to Michigan). While my grandfather Austin had gone to Brown, there was no continuing family tie to it. There seemed to be no particular pull from any of these previous family *alma maters*, so I started on a new search.

My father had an editorial source and friend who had been a professor at Columbia in New York City: Raymond Moley, one of the key members of President Roosevelt's "Brains Trust." Would Columbia be a candidate for me? Well, it was in a very big city, and that sort of scared me.

My father had a friend from Ohio State who was a celebrated historian at Harvard—Arthur Schlesinger, Sr. (whose son, Arthur, Jr., would later become the leading historian of the New Deal era). So we stopped to visit him while on a trip to New England, and Harvard was a possibility for me. I had classmates at Western High School who were interested in Amherst, and they asked me to go up with them for a visit. It was quiet and beautiful, but it seemed somewhat removed from the hurly burly of the life I had been accustomed to.

In Washington and public life in the early New Deal days, there seemed to be quite a few people with Cornell connections. The governor of the Farm Credit Administration, William I. Myers, was a Cornell graduate and former dean of agriculture at Cornell. He was an editorial source for my father. The governor of New York State, Herbert Lehman, who succeeded Franklin D. Roosevelt in that post, was a trustee of Cornell. And the Secretary of the Treasury, Henry Morgenthau, Jr., one of my father's sources on financial affairs, turned out to be a Cornell graduate, too—but not in finance or government; he had graduated from Cornell's New York State College of Agriculture. When my father called on him at his office one day, he casually mentioned that his son was getting ready to go to college, and he wondered if the secretary had any ideas on where he should go. Mr. Morgenthau, without hesitating, said, "Why, Cornell, of course."

Whether this had any influence on my decision, I don't know. I only know that when I visited Cornell University, it piqued my interest, with its broad mixture of liberal arts, practical studies, Ivy League traditions, Land Grant origins, and students from every walk of life, studying disciplines from architecture to government to music. It seemed like a diverse society, like the whole United States that I would be writing about in my likely future profession of journalism. It appealed to me even as a 16-year-old student from Washington, D.C.

So, now it was 1935, and I was a freshman at Cornell. Roosevelt was in his first term as President of the United States. The New Deal was proclaiming a broadened role for government in people's lives. Around the world, from Germany to Italy to China, nations were struggling with problems of survival amid a severe global depression. People were searching for new models of society, ranging from democracy to various models of totalitarianism.

The most strident voice in the totalitarian camp was that of Hitler, that strangely hypnotizing little man with the moustache whom Charlie Chaplin would satirize in his tragicomic movie "The Great Dictator" a few years later. But Hitler was no laughing matter. By the time I entered college, he was already throwing dissidents in prison and beginning his persecution of Jews, proclaiming his bogus theory of Aryan superiority. The question for political leaders in the western world was how to cope with this menace.

The year after I finished at Cornell, a Harvard student named John F. Kennedy wrote a senior thesis that lambasted British leaders—especially Prime Minister Neville Chamberlain—for being complacent about the rise of Hitler and entering into the Munich Pact with the dictator, heralding "peace in our time." Kennedy's powerful father, Joseph P. Kennedy, then U.S. ambassador to Great

Britain, arranged for his son's thesis to be published as a book, *Why England Slept,* which became a national best-seller in 1940.

We Americans had long been ignoring the threat of Hitler, Mussolini and Japan much more than the Europeans had. Isolationism was the prevailing attitude in the U.S., right up to Pearl Harbor. Even a "holier than thou" form of pacifism was popular. Antiwar activist Sen. Gerald P. Nye (R-N.D.) railed against U.S. involvement in "European rivalries" and condemned the du Ponts of Delaware as "merchants of death." (Senator Nye's daughter had sat next to me in high school, and she seemed normal enough.) Racism and anti-Semitism were swept under the rug in polite society, or merely dismissed as exaggerations. Some of my college friends came home from summer travel in Germany with an admiration for the vigor of German youth, and they credited Mussolini and Hitler with "making the trains run on time."

Student Factions

I was exposed to all of these attitudes, but I wasn't comfortable with them. I gradually became an internationalist—an interventionist favoring American involvement in the European crisis, to support the democracies against Fascism. (My father, who didn't take sides or advocate policies in his *Kiplinger Washington Letter*, continually predicted in the mid '30s that that there would be war in Europe in a few years and that the U.S. would eventually be drawn into it, like it or not).

My friends at Cornell ran the gamut from conservative isolationists to Communists who favored aggressive opposition to the Fascist dictators (but who didn't seem troubled by excesses of Stalin, whom some of them idealized.) Like many young liberals of the era, I was skeptical of ideologies. In 1937, I helped form the Campus Peace Council, and our supporters ranged from passionate pacifists to others—like me—who believed that the best way to prevent war and defend democracy was to be militarily prepared.

In the summer of 1938, I traveled to Europe again, not with my father this time, but with my close Cornell friend Bob Cline, who was Jewish. We knew about Hitler's growing aggression throughout Europe, and we were curious to see Nazi Germany for ourselves. But after just one day in Hamburg, where brown-shirted storm troopers were a chilling presence everywhere, we had seen enough. We quickly left.

For college leftists, the ultimate shock came in August of 1939, a few months after I finished at Cornell and was about to start graduate study in economics at Harvard. Stalin and Hitler entered into a non-aggression pact, pledging not to attack each other. In the following month, Hitler's tanks conquered Poland from the west, while the Soviets seized the eastern part of that nation. World War II had started.

On the campuses of American colleges, the Nazi-Soviet pact was a wake-up call and disillusionment. Young liberals suddenly comprehended the facts of real politics—the bare knuckle politics of power. It was now clear who were disciplined Communists and who were liberal idealists. The Young Communist League suddenly became pitted against the American Student Union and other liberal campus groups. Radical young Communists who had long denounced Hitler suddenly became hands-off isolationists, and—taking their cue from Moscow—apologists for dictatorial regimes. U.S. intervention in Europe, in support of England and France, became the touchstone for the young liberals, separating them from card-carrying Communists.

When the turbulent decade of the Thirties came to an end, talk turned to action. After Pearl Harbor, many intellectual opponents found themselves on the same side, wearing the military uniforms of the United States.

After College

I don't know how and where all the campus firebrands I knew in the 1930s ended up. Some of them, but not all, left their student political views behind them. My roommate Frederick J. (Fritz) Rarig, once a vociferous Marxist, became a lawyer and worked for the U.S. government during World War II, helping take control of the American factories of a Swedish steel company that also owned plants in Nazi Germany. Rarig later became general counsel and a vice president of the huge chemical and plastics company, Rohm & Haas.

Another friend at Cornell, a Communist named Frank Untermyer, was a grandson of the illustrious and wealthy New York corporate lawyer Samuel Untermyer. Frank seemed terribly embarrassed, almost pained, by the fact of his grandfather's wealth, even though Untermyer was a leader of the campaign to impose a global boycott on Germany's exports, to undermine Hitler's regime. Frank, I found out later, served as an officer in the U.S. Army during World War II, and then became a professor of political science and African studies at Roosevelt University in Chicago. He was known as a champion of social justice and civil liberties.

I had a friend at Cornell named Ben Alexander, and one day in 1942, early in the war, I ran into him by chance on the streets of Washington. I was startled to see him in a Navy uniform, because in college he had been a fervent Communist, and I couldn't imagine him passing a security interview. But Ben was a special kind of Communist—a Leninist-Trotskyite who was bitterly opposed to Stalin for the dictator's perversion of the socialist ideal. "How did they ever let you into the Navy?" I asked Ben. "Well," he responded, "the recruiter asked me what I thought about Stalin, and I told him." I never learned what Alexander did with the rest of his life.

Another college-time acquaintance was William Remington, Dartmouth '39. He and I were co-chairmen of an inter-collegiate conference called "Making Democracy Work." Three colleges were involved—Dartmouth, Cornell and Pennsylvania. Remington was the Dartmouth chairman, I was chairman from Cornell, and the chairman from Penn was Reginald H. Jones (who spent his entire career with General Electric, rising to chairman of the board).

I had not kept in touch with Remington after college, but out of the blue, around 1947 or '48, he contacted me when I was working on our new *Kiplinger Magazine* in Washington. He had worked during and after World War II in Washington, in senior economics positions in the government, and he was under investigation on suspicion of having passed government secrets to an American woman, Elizabeth Bentley, who was a spy for the Soviets. He asked me if I would vouch for him, testifying that I hadn't known him to be a Communist back in our college days in the Thirties. I told him that I wasn't aware of his political leanings in that period, so I couldn't say anything useful one way or another. That was the last I heard from him. I later learned that he was convicted of perjury about having been a Communist activist during and after college and giving government information to Bentley. He was sent to federal prison, where he was murdered by an inmate in 1954.

The college political activism of the 1930s, like that of the 1960s, underscored a basic fact: When you have a wave of young people in the population, you can count on a lot of turmoil and change. But history also shows that the firmly held beliefs of youths will not always endure through the rest of their lives. Plato had something to say about it to Theaetetus: "You are young, my son, and as the years go by, time will change and even reverse some of your present opinions. Refrain awhile, therefore, from setting yourself up as a judge of the highest matters."

So, the next time we encounter a wave of campus tempest and turmoil, just remember that "this too shall pass"—and probably come back again.

6

You Gotta Getta Job

At the end of the 1930s, newspaper pay in the U.S. was notoriously low. The pall of depression still hung over the publishing world, and the low pay of newspapermen promoted the image of reporters as low-life bohemians who were perpetually "down at the heel." Economically speaking, this was basically true. In practice, it became a matter of making do on a very low income. A collateral fact of journalistic life was the shortage of new jobs. Nevertheless, for aspiring journalists, hope sprang eternal.

After a year of graduate study in economics at Harvard, I went looking for a full-time newspaper job in 1940. I didn't expect to make much money, but I did think I had good qualifications—for a beginner. I thought someone would jump at the chance to pick up some young talent cheap.

As far as the qualifications were concerned, beside my education and writing for student publications (editor of *Areopagus*, The Cornell Journal of Opinion), I had worked part-time as the Cornell campus stringer for the local daily, *The Ithaca Journal*, and for the Associated Press, which picked up a number of my stories for the New York State wire. And I had grown up around my father's editorial offices in Washington. So off I went in my quest for a job.

First call: the *Christian Science Monitor* in Boston, which was geographically closest on my list. At the newspaper office in the elegant "Mother Church" building, I was met by a dignified doorman who presented me personally to the managing editor, and I could hardly believe my eyes at how clean his office was. Even the newsroom was spotless (no crumpled paper on the floor) and quiet (no raucous conversation, no loud calls for "Copyboy!"). It was a dignified place, befitting the reputation of the paper. And the managing editor (later its longtime editor in chief) was a dignified man—Erwin Canham, known to his friends as "Spike," a respected newspaperman and a professional friend of my father. I presented my case. Mr. Canham listened calmly, complimented me on my qualifications, and wished me well—but no offer of a job.

Heading West

Next stop, New York—the big city itself—and *The New York Times*. Same scenario: respectful reception but no job. So I decided to head west. In Oklahoma City I got an appointment with the editor and publisher of the *Daily Oklahoman*. He agreed that I was a very promising prospect, but he wasn't putting anyone on the payroll right now. So, on to California. At the *Los Angeles Times*, my interview was with general manager (later editor and publisher) Norman Chandler, who was very flattering about my qualifications, but—you guessed it—no job.

Pasadena was close by, and there was a newspaper there too, the *Pasadena Star-News*, so I decided to try it. I knocked on the door of the general manager, who, I discovered, was married to the daughter of the publisher. But more impressive than that, he was the great Charlie Paddock, holder of the world's record in the 100-meter dash record and therefore "the world's fastest human." I was awed, but I presented my credentials, and he thought I might fit into their organization. First, though, I had to pass muster with his father-in-law, the publisher and owner, Charles H. Prisk. His office was at another paper he owned, the Long Beach *Press-Telegram*. So off to Long Beach, where the dignified Mr. Prisk spent a half hour quizzing me about my political philosophy, my attitude toward organized labor, and all the prickly issues of the day. As a fresh-faced young liberal just out of academia, I did my best to present a sober-sided, dispassionate view of all the issues of the day. But when it was over, Mr. Prisk decided that I was not sufficiently anti-union to pass his litmus test, so—again—no job.

One more chance in Los Angeles: the *Los Angeles Daily News*, a somewhat racy, liberal tabloid that nipped at the heels of the dominant, conservative *Times*. The publisher was Manchester Boddy, a colorful independent who ran the paper on a shoestring and ordered that it give balanced coverage to social causes and reforms that were ignored or ridiculed by other papers. (A decade later, in 1950, Boddy fought Rep. Helen Gahagan Douglas for the Democratic nomination for Senate. Though he lost, his portrayal of her as the "Pink Lady" who was soft on Communism weakened her badly, and it permitted the GOP nominee, Rep. Richard Nixon, to win the Senate seat.) We had a good visit, Mr. Boddy and I, and I was feeling optimistic, but then reality set in. He was still operating on a shoe-string, and he didn't have any budget for a new person on the staff, so no job.

A Job in San Francisco

I had just enough money for one more shot, and it would have to be in California, so I headed north to San Francisco. Now I would have to get a job—any job—but I hoped it would be on a newspaper.

In the city beside the Golden Gate, I decided to try to get an interview with the top editor of the *San Francisco Chronicle*, Paul C. Smith, 32 years old, the "boy wonder" of the newspaper world. An ambitious young man with little formal education but much worldly experience, he had been named business editor of the *Chronicle* at 24 and executive editor at 27, in 1935. (Three years later, he accepted an invitation from the longshoremen's union to serve as the outside mediator of a long and bitter strike on the San Francisco waterfront, helping secure a settlement.) I was awed by his reputation, but I called for an appointment anyway—and got one.

In Smith's office, we talked about Washington, national affairs and the war in Europe. Not much talk about newspaper experience, but after a while, Smith said, "I think we can use you. I think we can find a spot for you." I almost passed out—I could hardly believe it. But I listened, and he said, "In the beginning, it won't be on the daily news staff, but we have a weekly news review on Sunday, something like *TIME* magazine, and it's called *This World*." I listened and nodded. It didn't occur to me to ask about pay, but he said, "We'll start you at $16 a week."

I had a job! $16 a week! It sounded like a million bucks.

Now I needed a place to live. I walked toward Nob Hill looking for rooms to rent—up Mason Street, across Pine, a dozen blocks from the *Chronicle* offices. Finally I saw a sign: "room for rent, $4 a week." $4 a week! That's about all I had left, but that was enough, and I paid the first week's rent. I had a home.

The address was 817 Mason Street, just downhill from the Mark Hopkins and Fairmont hotels and their neighbor, the prestigious Pacific-Union Club, once the mansion of silver baron James C. Flood. But none of this was on my mind. The rent was reasonable because it was below an alley. And I had bathroom privileges after the landlords, a barber and his wife, had gone to work—not bad, since I liked to sleep later anyway. Out the window I could catch a glimpse of gray water (just a sliver), and I told everybody triumphantly that I had "a view of the Bay for $4 a week." Nobody else ever had it so good.

As I got into the routine, I would get my $16 a week pay, give my landlord $4 in advance and still have $12 to live on for the rest of the week. (I would pay my taxes later.) I decided to eat on $1 a day. Breakfast was an avocado, which I bought at the market for 10 cents. The lunchroom owner let me eat at the counter if I bought a glass of milk for 10 cents. (Breakfast, 20 cents.) Lunch at Breen's Saloon, down Market Street next to the *Examiner* (our newspaper rival, from Hearst). A fat turkey sandwich cost 25 cents and a glass of beer, 10 cents. (Total for lunch 35 cents.) That left 45 cents for dinner, which was fine.

If I stuck to this regimen (which I managed to do only part of the time), I would have $5 a week for "everything else," but through ingenuity and cajolery, a young reporter could live the good life on practically no money. Free theater tickets could be cadged from the drama desk. Concert tickets could be acquired through the generosity of Alfred Frankenstein, the *Chronicle's* music and art critic, whose desk was on the same floor as the city desk. For access to opera, I could sign up to "work" for Carolyn Anspacher, a former actress who was the paper's "sob sister," more formally known as the principal women's writer, specializing in heart-rending feature stories. We would cover the "who's who" arriving at the opera house in long gowns and white-tie-and-tails. (Anspacher's career at the *Chronicle* spanned 46 years, and her crime coverage—from the grisly San Jose lynchings in 1933 to the Patty Hearst kidnapping in 1974—was legendary.)

All this good living on $16 a week! Six months later, I received the biggest raise that I ever I got in my life—50%, from $16 to $24 a week! Never again did I get a 50 % raise, and never again did any raise ever feel so good.

The *Chronicle* Newsroom

The newsroom was an astonishing collection of young talent. Executive Editor Paul Smith was just 32. The managing editor, 30 years old, was Larry Fanning, who had started at the *Chronicle* as a teenaged copy boy and returned after college, becoming the ME at 26. (He was later editor of the *Chicago Daily News*, and ended up in 1966 as co-owner of the *Anchorage Daily News* with his new wife, Kay Woodruff Field Fanning, ex-wife of Marshall Field IV.) The editor of *This World*, the Sunday magazine, was Scott Newhall, age 26, who would succeed Smith as the *Chronicle*'s editor a decade later. (I worked alongside his journalist wife, Ruth Newhall, who was eight months' pregnant with their second child.) George de Carvalho, 19, was a copy-boy-turned-rewrite-man who, in 1952, would win a Pulitzer for the *Chronicle* in investigative reporting. Abe Mellinkoff, the assistant city editor who took no nonsense from anyone, was all of 27; he would spend his entire career at the *Chronicle*, as city editor and columnist.

Stanton Delaplane, already a star reporter and my mentor during Rice Bowl coverage in San Francisco and Fresno, was the old man of the staff—age 33. (The Rice Bowl festivals were fundraisers put on by Chinese-Americans to raise money for the beleaguered Chinese Nationalist government, which was fighting both the occupying Japanese and the communist insurgency.) Stan would stay at the *Chronicle* for a half century, winning a Pulitzer in 1942 and writing his famous "Postcards" travel column from his home on Telegraph Hill. One of his biggest reportorial coups was in 1940, when the *Chronicle* beat the competition on the capture of the kidnapper of three-year-old Marc de Tristan, Jr. Three days after the young Marc was snatched from his nanny outside the family's mansion in Hillsborough, down the peninsula from San Francisco, the *Chronicle*—and Stan Delaplane—were on the scene near Placerville, in the Gold Country of the Sierra Nevadas. The kidnapper, who had demanded $100,000 ransom, was captured by two lumbermen, and the little boy was rescued unharmed. Delaplane got the story first, and the *Chronicle* hit the streets with his scoop before the *Examiner* knew what had happened.

There were more bright young writers. Charlie Downie, 24, later edited for the *Stars and Stripes,* the Army newspaper in the European Theater, then stayed in Italy after the war to co-found the *Rome Daily American.* (In 1950 he returned to the *Chronicle* for good.) Gordon Pate, copy editor, taught me the difference between a "dock" and a "pier." He said that "a pier is what you walk on, and the dock is what the boat floats in." He clinched the lesson by asserting that "only one man in history ever walked on a dock; the rest of you walk on a pier."

The biggest name at the paper was Herb Caen, then only 24 but already a celebrated columnist. Paul Smith had hired him from the *Sacramento Union* four years earlier to write a radio column for the *Chronicle,* and Caen had started his inimitable nightlife and human interest column two years after that, becoming the must-read chronicler of all things San Francisco.

The *Chronicle* was the Newspaper Guild (union) paper, and Smith wanted it to be honest, sophisticated, well-written and classy, like *The New York Times.* It didn't make much money. The *Examiner*, on the other hand, was William Randolph Hearst's first big newpaper, the jewel in his crown. It was gossipy, and everybody read it. It covered The City by the Bay, and San Franciscans loved it. They said they read the *Chronicle* for "serious subjects," but the *Examiner* was their meat. The *Chronicle* was their alibi. (When Scott Newhall took over the *Chronicle* in the 1950s, he made it a more popular, folksy read, and it soared in circulation. Eventually it overtook the *Examiner* as the most widely read paper in San Francisco.)

General Assignment Reporter

In 1940, we at the *Chronicle*, bright young prodigies that we were, soldiered on, telling San Francisco about the world…and the war that would soon be upon them.

Presumably, nothing you ever learn will be wasted, but I am still waiting to use the information I learned as a rewrite man on *This World*. At that time, I became the world's greatest expert on the Greek-Albanian war– officially known today as Greco-Italian War of 1940-'41. I was assigned to "cover" the war…7,000 miles away. Even now I can regale an unsuspecting listener with details about Greece's colorful Evzone mountain troops in their leather clogs with black pompons on the toes, and I can speak familiarly about the Albanian cities of Argyrokastro and Tirana. (Tirana, I was told, was named after the Persian city of Tehran by the troops of Cyrus the Great, who conquered the area around 550 B.C.)

After three months of rewrite on *This World*, I received a transfer to "city side," where I began reporting under assistant city editor Mellinkoff.

In October, 1940 Western Europe had been overrun by Hitler, but the United States remained strongly isolationist. Around San Francisco, one of the loudest voices for continued American non-intervention was Dr. Ray Lyman Wilbur, M.D., the president of Stanford who had served as President Herbert Hoover's Interior Secretary (simultaneous with his college presidency). He was a critic of the Roosevelt administration, and during a conference at the university, I heard him criticize the drafting of young Americans.

A month later, I reported his speech before the San Francisco Commonwealth Club, in which he said, "There's no greater stupidity than for this country to fight against Japan or anybody else." He criticized Roosevelt's Lend-Lease aid for the democracies of Western Europe as an example of Washington's "centralization and tyranny." I didn't agree with his views, but I dutifully reported what he said.

My assignments ran the gamut from frivolous features about "Tombstone," the San Francisco Press Club cat, to grim reports from European visitors such as Dr. Paul Van Zeeland, the former prime minister of Belgium, whose country had been overrun by the Germans. Food was so scarce in Belgium, he said, "children are fainting in the schools." A week earlier I had reported the remarks of Sen. Gerald P. Nye (R-N.D), who told me in an interview that, because of the Lend-Lease partnership with Britain, "Germany would be justified in declaring war on us today." (Senator Nye had greeted me warmly, because, as I noted earlier, I had been a classmate of his daughter at Western High School in Washington.) So strong was the American isolationist feeling, even in San Francisco, that Senator Nye was cordially received by Mayor Angelo Rossi and enthusiastically introduced to a full-house crowd at the Civic Auditorium—all this just a year before the Japanese attack on Pearl Harbor.

As required by law, I signed up for the draft at the Selective Service office in downtown San Francisco, but our district housed so many single men that one wag suggested we would never be called for military duty until Gabriel blew his horn.

My news assignments continued to include everything from local rooming-house murders to interviewing international visitors. In February of 1941, I covered a Stanford symposium at which Prof. Karl Brandt, an anti-Nazi German expatriate and noted agricultural economist, said that Hitler's food supplies were sufficient for the German juggernaut to invade England within three months. As it turned out, Hitler's plan was thwarted by the Royal Air Force in the Battle of Britain, and Germany's troops never crossed the English Channel.

When any delegation of federal officials arrived from Washington, I got the reporting assignment. Thurman Arnold, a former Yale Law School professor, came to San Francisco in his new position as Assistant Attorney General for antitrust policy. (Carrying his briefcase was his assistant Tom C. Clark, who later served as Attorney General and a justice of the Supreme Court.)

After interviewing Arnold at the Palace Hotel, I reported that he believed the antitrust laws did not conflict with national defense and would not hamper rearming the nation. (A year later, after the Japanese attack on Pearl Harbor, antitrust laws were virtually suspended to permit the U.S. economy to be consolidated for war production.)

A Mock Enlistment

As more young men began lining up at military recruiting offices, the *Chronicle* widened its coverage of national defense, and I was given an assignment to do a feature on enlisting. I paid a visit to the Navy recruiting office, accompanied by Clem Albers, the *Chronicle*'s senior photographer, for a Sunday feature on getting into the Navy. So, in January, 1941, a full-page feature appeared, chronicling the enlistment process, replete with information forms, interrogations, police check-up and physical exam. (In the accompanying photos, a skinny Austin Kiplinger was shown in his underwear.) I passed the mock enlistment, and the petty officer was disappointed that it wasn't for real. "It would do you good," he said.

Most of my assignments were free of violence and mayhem, but I did draw an occasional tour of police reporting, with its quota of tawdry murders, drunken arrests, drownings and kidnappings. And I learned something very telling: Any police reporter can create a "crime wave" by simply reporting, as a matter of fact, everything that happened on his beat that day.

It was 1941. Hitler was on a rampage in Europe, the Japanese were marauding through China and Indo-China, and the West Coast reading public was hungry for on-the-scene news from the Orient. One morning when things were quiet at the *Chronicle*, Gordon Pate called me over to the city desk. "I've got a question for you," he said. "How would you like to go to Shanghai?" My heart started to pound and I said I'd be interested, but how? Well, he said, he had an offer from a friend on the *North China Daily News*, an English-language paper, who needed two experienced reporters, ready to go to work. If I said yes, he and I would leave as soon as possible. I was ecstatic, and I reported it to City Editor Mellinkoff. He was amenable to giving me a leave, but he reminded me that I needed to notify my draft board. I assumed that was just a formality and I proceeded to do so. The draft board spokesman looked at me coldly and said, "You are under the jurisdiction of the draft system. You are on call for military service. You're not leaving the country." There was no arguing with him. Pate and I were stymied; we notified the *North China Daily News* that we were not coming.

Back to D.C.

Then another call came...this one from Washington. It was from my father, editor of *The Kiplinger Washington Letter*. He needed help, he said. He had agreed with Cass Canfield, the legendary head of Harper & Brothers publishers in New York, to write a comprehensive book about Washington. He was up to his neck in work with his *Letter*, in addition to free-lance writing for *The New York Times Sunday Magazine*. He wanted to do the book, but he would need to recruit a staff of writers to help with research and reporting. And he needed a "chief of staff" to ride herd. Would I do it?

I said yes.

I had traveled the country looking for work.

I had gotten a job in San Francisco.

I had gotten a 50% raise.

And now I had another job—in Washington.

Austin Kiplinger on right, with his father, W.M. Kiplinger in the garden at family home on River Road in Bethesda, Summer, 1942, when Austin was a Naval Aviation cadet

Workforce of the Miller Carriage Co., Bellefontaine, Ohio circa 1885. Great-grandfather Amos Miller, far right, holding bowler hat. Grandfather Clarence Kiplinger, top row, second from left

House at 721 Shepherd St., Washington, D.C. where Austin Kiplinger's parents were living when he was born on September 19, 1918 (his mother is seated on the front steps)

Message filed by Austin Kiplinger to the San Francisco Chronicle after Pearl Harbor attack. It appeared the next morning on page one of the Chronicle in San Francisco

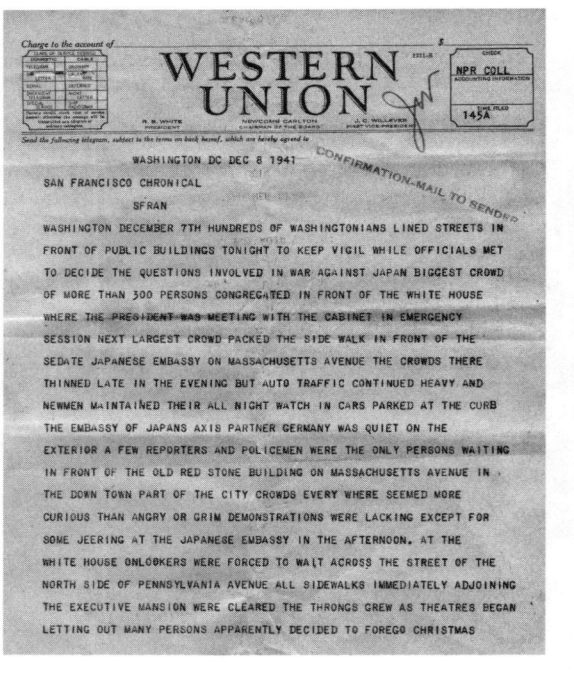

WASHINGTON DC DEC 8 1941

SAN FRANCISCO CHRONICAL
SFRAN

WASHINGTON DECEMBER 7TH HUNDREDS OF WASHINGTONIANS LINED STREETS IN FRONT OF PUBLIC BUILDINGS TONIGHT TO KEEP VIGIL WHILE OFFICIALS MET TO DECIDE THE QUESTIONS INVOLVED IN WAR AGAINST JAPAN BIGGEST CROWD OF MORE THAN 300 PERSONS CONGREGATED IN FRONT OF THE WHITE HOUSE WHERE THE PRESIDENT WAS MEETING WITH THE CABINET IN EMERGENCY SESSION NEXT LARGEST CROWD PACKED THE SIDE WALK IN FRONT OF THE SEDATE JAPANESE EMBASSY ON MASSACHUSETTS AVENUE THE CROWDS THERE THINNED LATE IN THE EVENING BUT AUTO TRAFFIC CONTINUED HEAVY AND NEWMEN MAINTAINED THEIR ALL NIGHT WATCH IN CARS PARKED AT THE CURB THE EMBASSY OF JAPANS AXIS PARTNER GERMANY WAS QUIET ON THE EXTERIOR A FEW REPORTERS AND POLICEMEN WERE THE ONLY PERSONS WAITING IN FRONT OF THE OLD RED STONE BUILDING ON MASSACHUSETTS AVENUE IN THE DOWN TOWN PART OF THE CITY CROWDS EVERY WHERE SEEMED MORE CURIOUS THAN ANGRY OR GRIM DEMONSTRATIONS WERE LACKING EXCEPT FOR SOME JEERING AT THE JAPANESE EMBASSY IN THE AFTERNOON. AT THE WHITE HOUSE ONLOOKERS WERE FORCED TO WAIT ACROSS THE STREET OF THE NORTH SIDE OF PENNSYLVANIA AVENUE ALL SIDEWALKS IMMEDIATELY ADJOINING THE EXECUTIVE MANSION WERE CLEARED THE THRONGS GREW AS THEATRES BEGAN LETTING OUT MANY PERSONS APPARENTLY DECIDED TO FOREGO CHRISTMAS

Dec. 29, 1948

The Round Table
By AUSTIN KIPLINGER

MR. ECCLES AND MR. SALTZ TALK PRICES

A conversation that took place in Washington last week throws a sharp light on some of the difficulties underlying the shift from a sellers' to a buyers' market.

The conversation was between Marriner Eccles and a Washington businessman. Eccles is the powerful member of the Federal Reserve Board (its former chairman) and the businessman is Lewis Saltz, who with his brother runs a haberdashery that caters to many of Washington's top officials.

The conversation took place in Mr. Saltz's store where Mr. Eccles had come to buy some pre-Christmas wearing apparel, and the talk ran like this:

MR. ECCLES: You'd better watch your inventories, Lewis. Things may be softening up.

MR. SALTZ: You know, Mr. Eccles, I have great respect for your judgement, but what do you expect retailers like us to do? Our costs are higher than ever, and people are still buying. What do you mean by softening up?

MR. ECCLES: I mean prices, Lewis. A lot of those goods market.

MR. SALTZ: I'll tell you about that. We've already bought our suits for next spring and summer. We've paid the going price, so we can't bring down the prices of good wool suits much. In addition we've paid a wage increase to our CIO tailors. Our other costs of doing business are higher than this time last year, so we've got to charge these prices.

MR. ECCLES: Well, maybe so, Lewis, but just the same, you'd better watch those inventories, because fellows like Marriner

(To page 8)

Austin Kiplinger Starts Today As New Author of Round Table

Starting today, a new by-line—that of Austin Kiplinger—appears on the Round Table, this paper's front-page commentary on business and national affairs.

Wilbur J. Brons, who has written the Round Table for the last five years, will continue to be the chief editorial writer of the Chicago Journal of Commerce. He will devote his entire time to supervision of the paper's editorial page. He remains the paper's top authority, other than the publisher, on editorial policy and opinion.

The Round Table has been a distinctive feature of the Chicago Journal of Commerce for more than 25 years. Less than two years after the paper's founding in 1920, the column was started by Glenn Griswold, who later became editor and publisher of Business Week and is now publisher of Public Relations News. Phil S. Hanna, now a business writer for the Chicago Daily News, wrote the Round Table in the 1930s.

Mr. Kiplinger came from Washington, D.C., to join our staff. He was associated there with his father, W.M. Kiplinger, publisher of Kiplinger's Letter. In 1945 he helped found Kiplinger's Magazine, a monthly, serving until recently as that publication's managing editor and executive editor. He is a graduate of Cornell University and did graduate work in economics at Harvard.

During the war Mr. Kiplinger was a Navy-torpedo-plane pilot in the Pacific. Before that he was a reporter and wrote news reviews for the San Francisco Chronicle.

The Round Table
(From page 1)

Eccles may not want to go on paying these prices forever.

* * *

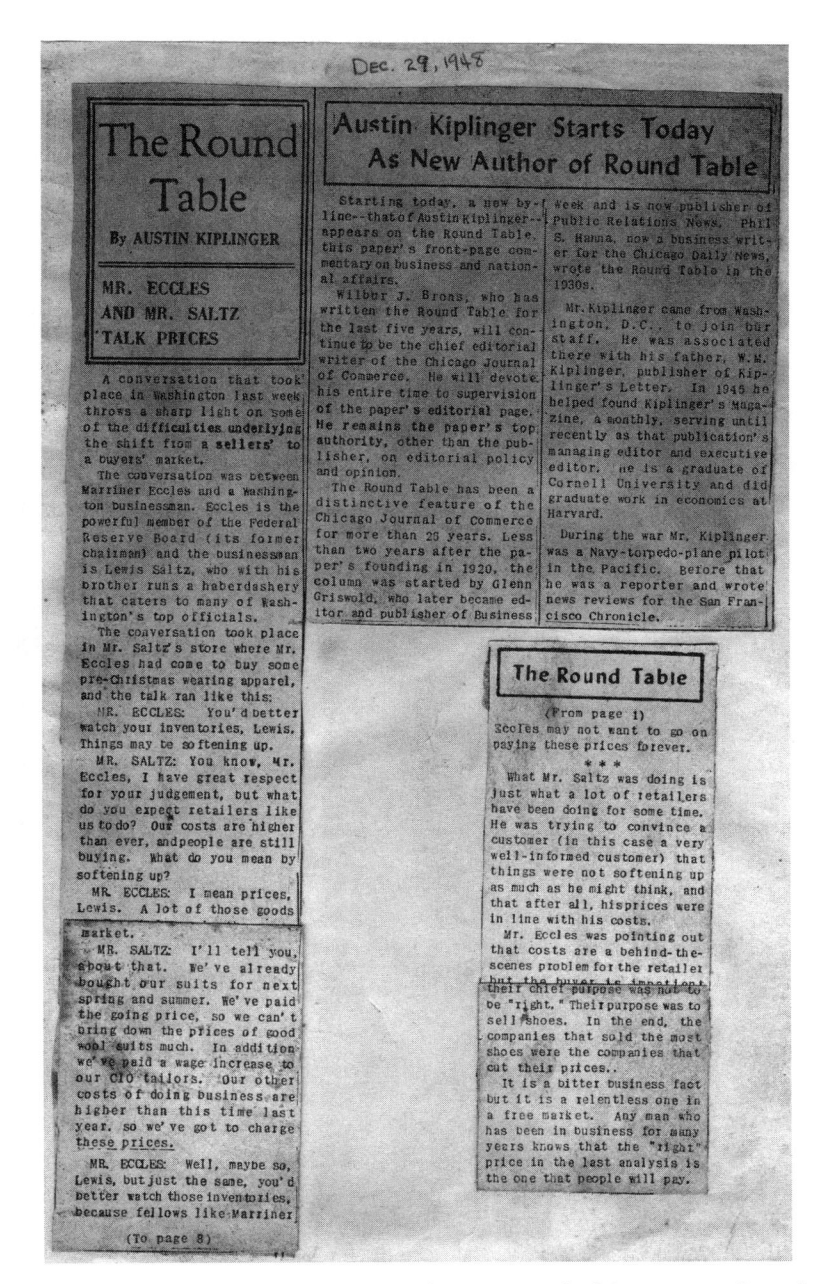

What Mr. Saltz was doing is just what a lot of retailers have been doing for some time. He was trying to convince a customer (in this case a very well-informed customer) that things were not softening up as much as he might think, and that after all, his prices were in line with his costs.

Mr. Eccles was pointing out that costs are a behind-the-scenes problem for the retailer but the buyer is important. Their chief purpose was not to be "right." Their purpose was to sell shoes. In the end, the companies that sold the most shoes were the companies that cut their prices.

It is a bitter business fact but it is a relentless one in a free market. Any man who has been in business for many years knows that the "right" price in the last analysis is the one that people will pay.

Austin Kiplinger's first column in the Chicago Journal of Commerce, featuring a conversation with the former Chairman of the Federal Reserve Board, 1948

Family portrait, 1926, Austin Kiplinger seated, with his father, W.M. Kiplinger at left, and Austin's grandparents, Cora and Clarence Kiplinger, 1926

CORNELL JOURNAL OF OPINION

AREOPAGUS

Cornell Student Council in Austin Kiplinger's senior year. Kiplinger, seated second left from speaker was Editor of the Areopagus Magazine and V-P of the Student Council

Let's Get A Few Things Straight
By WALT H. FOERTSCH

VOL. VII, No. 1   Price 10c   OCTOBER, 1938

Staff of Kiplinger Letter, National Press Building, Circa 1943 L-R: Morgan, Covel, Shelton, Granducci, Kiplinger (center), Wright, Mullin, Ryerson

Austin Kiplinger, holding 40th anniversary issue of the
Kiplinger Magazine, Changing Times, of which he was
Executive Editor when it first appeared in 1947

Logo of Austin Kiplinger's award-winning TV show, Impact, in Chicago, 1952

USS Nassau (CVE 16), Squadron VC 66s first combat ship en route to Marshall Islands campaign, Jan-Feb. 1944

Pilots at Naval Air Station, Fort Lauderdale, Fla., training in the first Grumman TBFs (torpedo bombers) 1943. Ensign Kiplinger front row, second from left

Cornell Student Council Committee Chairman 1938-39 Austin Kiplinger in top row, fourth from the right

Austin Kiplinger, with short-term mustache, in early offices of the proposed Kiplinger Magazine, Washington, D.C., 1946

Austin Kiplinger's 6 o'clock TV news, Chicago, 1952. Election Night Returns, Adlai Stevenson, Dwight Eisenhower

Austin Kiplinger at the console of an IBM 370/158 at the Editors Park publishing offices of the Kiplinger Washington Editors 1973

Three generations of Kiplinger Washington Editors

84

7

Time Out for War

For many of the people on earth, World War II began long before the United States entered the war at the end of 1941. For millions of Chinese, it began when Japan invaded Manchuria in 1931. For Ethiopians, it came in 1935, when Mussolini's Italian army invaded their country. For the Czechs, it was when Hitler seized their country in 1938, calling it the Sudetenland of Germany. For the Poles, Dutch, Belgians and French, war came when Hitler's tanks rolled across Europe in 1939 and '40, and then invaded Russia in the summer of 1941.

U.S. relations with Japan grew more and more tense through 1941. Knowledgeable people in Washington were expecting some kind of triggering event that would lead to open warfare between the two nations, although no one knew where or when it would come. On Dec. 6, 1941, the day before the attack on Pearl Harbor, *The Kiplinger Washington Letter* closed with these lines:

<u>War with Japan</u>? Officials as late as this afternoon, Saturday, simply did not know, but their cautious private observations indicated that they are prepared for the worst.

On Sunday, the day after this *Letter* was put in the mail, the weather in Washington was unseasonably warm. I decided to take a break from my editorial duties, working on the book about Washington, and take a drive in the country. I asked my grandmother if she would like to come along. We went out River Road, past Potomac and into the Maryland countryside beyond Great Falls, just ambling around and basking in the sunny warmth.

In the late afternoon we drove back to my father's home in Bethesda, and we found it in an uproar. Pearl Harbor had been attacked! The U.S. was at war!

The U.S. at War

My father said, "Let's go," and we piled into the car to drive to our office downtown in the National Press Building. We talked about what we would do. The week's *Letter* was already in the mail, but work began on the next, which would focus entirely on the conversion of a civilian economy to wartime production. My assignment was to redo large portions of the book that my father and I were writing, *Washington is Like That*. But I would not be able to reach our contributors until morning, so I contacted my former editor on the San Francisco *Chronicle*, from which I was on leave of absence. Scott Newhall, editor of *This World*, the *Chronicle*'s Sunday magazine, said they were getting all the hard news they needed from the wire services, but they could use a little "color" from Washington.

I walked over to the White House, three blocks away. Lights were shining from every window. People were gathered along the front fence. There was an air of foreboding and bewilderment. To the west, at the War Department, the scene was the same. Ditto at the Navy Department on Constitution Avenue. I wrote a "mood piece" and filed it to San Francisco, where it appeared on page one of the *Chronicle* on Monday morning:

"Hundreds of Washingtonians lined streets in front of public buildings tonight to keep vigil while officials met to decide the questions involved in war against Japan...The biggest crowd congregated in front of the White House, where the President was meeting with the Cabinet in emergency session..."

My mind flashed back to the mood of the past few years. The issue of American involvement was a constant topic in every social, academic or casual conversation. Tension between otherwise friendly Americans was severe on "intervention" versus "isolation," comparable to the later public uproar in the 1950s surrounding "McCarthyism." I recalled a 1936 interview I had done for the *Ithaca Journal* with Dr. Hu Shih, a Cornell alumnus who was then a leading education reformer in China and later (1938-'42) China's ambassador to the U.S. and, after the war, chancellor of Peking University. "In the absence of almost miraculous world leadership," he told me, the invasion of China by the Japanese would lead to a general world war.

I remembered when I visited Germany in 1938 as a student and saw Nazi Brown Shirts goose-stepping in the streets of Hamburg. I had felt at the time that would be no hiding place for Americans, and that someday, "the war" would soon be "our war."

I recalled the day two years earlier, in September 1939, when Hitler attacked Poland and I was a graduate student at Harvard studying economics. I knew that I would not have time to complete my master's degree in economics, and that, sooner or later, I would be in a military uniform. So I decided to leave after a year of study and get started in my intended profession of journalism, leading me eventually to San Francisco. I also decided that when I did go into military service, I would be in the air, not on the ground. My old school friend, Lewis Gordon, had become a Naval aviator flying F4U fighters in the Marines, and he had convinced me that was the way to go.

Learning to Fly

Now the United States had been attacked, and we were at war. So I went to the Naval recruiting office, in the Old Post Office Building on Pennsylvania Avenue, and signed up for training as a Navy pilot. But because of the logjam of recruits, I was not called until April, and then I reported the next month to the Anacostia Naval Air Station in Washington, across the river from the old Navy Yard that the British had burned in 1814. I was duly finger-printed, photographed, given the requisite physical exam, and enlisted in the United States Navy as a seaman second-class student naval aviator. At least I was one level above apprentice seaman.

The next 20 months were the standard Naval Air training, learning to fly from land—in daylight and at night, in clear weather and fog—and at sea from aircraft carriers. Twenty months to produce a combat-ready aviator, not the least of which was the trick of flying off Navy ships and somehow getting back aboard them. The Army Air Corps was turning out combat pilots for war in

Europe in less than a year, and some of them were coming back with a chest full of ribbons. In fact, it was sometimes a source of envy for us Navy aviators who had opted to fly at sea, but we understood the imperatives of different kinds of warfare. For us, there were no muddy airfields. But there was the always-present prospect of hitting the water and going straight down—no mess, no fuss, just a quick and clean end. It was a trade-off that we fully understood.

As for the differential between training times—land-based versus sea-based aviation—this too was something we came to understand and come to terms with. Landing aboard a ship called for special techniques. Our carrier would be 400 feet long, and only half of that was available for landings—the front end of the flight deck was needed for parking planes. Carrier landing training would be constant—from Pensacola, Fla., to Glenview, Ill., over Lake Michigan, at almost every Naval air station along the Atlantic and Pacific coasts of the U.S., plus shake-down cruises aboard the carriers *Wolverine* (on Lake Michigan), *Tripoli, Manila Bay* and *Nassau* (in the Pacific Ocean).

There was navigation to be learned—"dead reckoning"—and the ubiquitous plotting board, which consisted of figuring your actual position after factoring in ship's speed and direction with your own air speed, direction and wind drift, adjusted by compass variations created by magnetic differences from true north.

It sounds like gobbledygook, but pilots who didn't learn it didn't come back. It took time, and there were other skills to learn: bombing (aerial drops and depth charges), the launching of torpedoes, the firing of machine guns, the tricks of air evasion, control of engines, and an infinite number of ways of making your plane do what you wanted it to. With all that came instrument training—learning to fly in darkness and fog. Seattle was the greatest place for learning to fly in fog...Puget Sound provided plenty of it. Night flying training was over the deserts of Southern California—out of Holtville and Indio and Thermal, with flights to Yuma, Ariz. and the Mexican border. At Otay Mesa, near San Diego, you could take off at the end of the runway and instantly be 300 feet above the ocean. At Thermal, you *had* to fly at night, because the daytime temperatures made the cowling of the plane too hot to touch.

Around Seattle, if you climbed high enough through the fog, you could take a sight on Mt. Rainier or Mount St. Helens at 10,000 and 12,000-ft altitudes. The problem was getting back down again without running into something like another plane, a radio tower or a mountain on the Olympic Peninsula. Practice in dropping torpedoes took place over Puget Sound out of Whidbey Island, where you were ordered *never* to fly under the high steel arch of the Deception Pass Bridge, near Anacortes. (I thought about the penalties every time I did it.) From Fort Lauderdale, on the southeast coast of Florida, you could practice by patrolling for German submarines that plied the shipping lanes off the East Coast of the United States.

To the Pacific

Finally, when you were ready to report to the fleet at North Island, San Diego, you heard that you were bound for Pearl Harbor, Hawaii, and you shouted for joy. We were champing at the bit. It was 1944, and the mid-Pacific was where the action was, and we were soon to be in it. Adding to our joy was the fact that our new orders canceled our original orders that would have sent us to the Aleutian Islands in Alaska, where the place was covered with snow and the water temperature was only a few degrees about freezing.

The Hawaiian ports were jammed. The airfields were crowded with planes. The bases and BOQs (bachelor officer quarters) were overrun with pilots, deck officers, destroyer crews, submariners—every rank and size and all eager to be called. Toothbrushes and shaving kits were at the ready.

Our squadron, VC-66, went aboard the USS *Nassau* (CVE-16) at Ford Island in Pearl Harbor, where the ship was anchored at a berth immediately above the sunken hull of the old battleship *Utah*, which had been hit by the Japanese attack on December 7, 1941. On the morning that we were due to sail, the entire ship's company was assembled on the hangar deck, and we dutifully waited to hear what was going to happen. Suddenly without warning, a deafening explosion rent the air, the ship heaved and rocked, we were thrown to our knees, and we thought we were under attack. We lept to our feet and ran topside, gathered in clumps and expected to hear orders to don life vests and abandon ship. But nothing came...no orders, no explanation. Finally the bullhorn sounded from the bridge. "Return to places. Secure all stations. Resume your duty. " That was all. Only later did we found out what it was all about. The hull of the sunken *Utah* was being dynamited, to turn it over and bring it to the surface after we sailed.

Marshall Islands Campaign

With the war going America's way, the Navy was moving westward, attempting to reclaim Japanese-occupied Pacific Islands (especially the Philippines) and edge ever-closer to Japan itself. Squadron VC-66 was anxiously awaiting action. As we steamed out of Pearl Harbor in January of 1944, word came that the Pacific Fleet was moving against the Japanese in the Marshall Islands, the biggest enemy military installation closest to the Hawaiian Islands. The Japanese had fortified the Marshalls in defiance of the mandate granted them by the League of Nations years before.

Five days later, when we came into view of the atoll of Majuro, we were at the south end of the Marshall Islands and nearly 200 miles from the fierce battles at Kwajalein. The atoll was a thing of beauty: the most breathtaking natural harbor we had ever seen. Our first action consisted of little more than sinking some rusty barges, but our next assignment was to neutralize the atolls of Wotje and Maloelap (with its Taroa Island), which were heavily fortified with airfields that could launch swarms of fighters and bombers against our fleet and our forces to the north. Every day, we put craters in the runways of those airfields, and the next morning the Japanese would have them filled and ready to use again.

Wotje Atoll and Taroa Island were about an hour's flying time from our ship, the *Nassau*. Accompanied by F4F Grumman Wildcat fighters, our TBF Grumman Avengers were launched by catapult, loaded with 500-lb bombs. The targets appeared in the distance like little rings of pearls. We all felt some palpitations, the kind that come to men who are about to go into combat for the first time. Our formation was led by Executive Officer Gerry Trapp, a fighter pilot, and when we reached Taroa he ordered the F4F fighters to commence strafing ahead of the TBF bombers. When the fighters had pulled up, we TBFs started our run, pushed over and began descent—a 45-degree dive called "glide bombing." Anti-aircraft fire was getting thicker. Fighters had stirred up a hornet's nest, and as I lined up on the main runway ahead, I put the target in my sights and reached for the bomb release lever. Then I felt a rapid series of sharp thuds. I was catching some hits from anti-aircraft fire but the cockpit had not been hit. The crew reported that they were not injured. I radioed Trapp that we had been hit. His question: "Can you still fly?" I thought we could, and we were now nearing the dropping point, so I pressed the electric button to drop the 500-pounders, and to make sure, I gave a yank on the manual release. The airfields were in a cloud of bomb dust as we pulled up to altitude, rendezvoused and headed back toward Majuro and the *Nassau*.

The fighters, with more speed, flew ahead and were landing as we TBFs made our approach. Lt. Joe Klaus, senior torpedo plane pilot, took his section in first, while we circled overhead. Following him, I let down into the landing pattern and onto the final approach. Chugging up the groove, I thought the plane felt heavier than it should after dropping 2,000 pounds of bombs, but I cocked the plane up into the approach attitude, with the propeller in low pitch and the mixture rich. Things seemed fine. The landing signal officer gave me a cut and I caught an early wire, stopping short of the barrier. Out of the corner of my eye, I saw the LSO (landing signal officer) dive into his safety net—a strange behavior—and now I noticed something else strange: The deck was deserted; not a soul was in sight. I was back from combat action and nobody was on deck. It was a deserted ship. Then, above the catwalk railing, a head slowly appeared, and then an ordnance man started running toward my plane. He was gesturing wildly, signaling for me to stay right where I was. I could hear him shout, "Don't Move!" He disappeared under the fuselage of my plane, and we waited.

Finally the ordnanceman came out from under the plane with a big smile. He climbed up on the wing, leaned in the cockpit and said, "It's OK now." "What's OK?" I asked. "The bombs," he said, "I've disarmed them." I said, "The bombs? I dropped them." He replied, "No, you didn't; your bomb bay doors were only half open. The bombs were lying loose in the bottom of the bomb bay, fully armed, ready to go off."

Slowly the story emerged. When we were hit by anti-aircraft fire, the strike knocked out the hydraulic line to the bomb bays, so the doors had only half opened when I pushed the electronic button. When I pulled the manual release, the bombs dropped from their hangers into the half-opened bomb bay. As the propellers in the nose cones of the bombs were windmilling on the homeward flight, the bombs armed themselves. By the time we got back, the bombs were ready to go off. If I had I made a bad landing, missed a wire or hit the barrier; we all would have been blown to Kingdom Come. The topside of the U.S.S. *Nassau* and everyone around it would have been destroyed. A hundred American families would have gotten that dreaded telegram.

Yet it was all in a day's work, and now heads began to pop up above the catwalk. The deck crew moved my plane forward. Orders were given to resume landings. The ship that had come within an inch of being demolished was receiving planes again and getting ready for the next action.

Back in Hawaii

After the battle of the Marshall Islands, we returned to Hawaii, spending time at Pearl Harbor on Oahu and at Barking Sands Field on the island of Kauai (so named for the crunching sound of its black lava sand under foot). Soon Squadron VC-66 was ordered to the airfield at Kahului, on the island of Maui, to await further assignment. It was July, 1944.

One morning we were abruptly shaken from sleep by loud-spoken orders for all pilots to report to the ready room—immediately! It was about 2 a.m., and in the ready room, we found our squadron skipper, Lt. Cdr. Herb Bragg, standing with some papers in his hand, but all he said was: "VT pilots, man your planes, tune up, keep idling and be ready for take-off. We'll give you further word when we have it." We asked, "What's going on?" and he said, "There's a report of unidentified ships coming in from the northeast." *Good God! Another Japanese attack? Incredible! But OK, let's get ready.* We weren't here on December 7, 1941, but this may be even bigger.

In full flight gear, life vests on, we waddled to the flight line, climbed onto the wing of our TBFs, and looked to the plane captains for signals to start engines. We all fired our engines and we waited.

The sky was dark, and in the still of an isolated airfield, we waited. All we had to do was get off the ground, fly in the dark, find that Japanese fleet and attack. We had torpedoes loaded aboard and engines were running. In fact, the engines of the TBFs were getting hot, and in a few minutes would have to be cut to avoid burning out. Still, no orders. My watch registered 3:15 a.m. If we were to make an attack before dawn, we should be in the air, but still no orders came.

Then in the earphones, a crackling order: "Cut engines. Secure your aircraft and return to ready room." Then we learned that the unidentified fleet was *ours*. It had been traveling under total secrecy, carrying President Franklin Roosevelt to a rendezvous with Fleet Adm. Chester Nimitz, commander of the entire Pacific Fleet—an extraordinary mid-ocean meeting to plot the attack on Japan.

Searching for Enemy Subs

In early 1944, the Japanese had pulled their surface fleet back toward their mainland and dispatched their submarines into the mid-Pacific to create havoc with our supply lines. Calling on experience the Navy had gained from the Atlantic fight against German submarines, Admiral Nimitz decided to activate an anti-submarine warfare program for squadrons in the Pacific, and VC-66 was the first squadron selected to take the refresher course at Kaneohe Bay on Oahu, in March of 1944. The plan called for anti-sub teams of one fighter and one torpedo plane working together. The TBF torpedo bomber was equipped with forward-firing 50-cal. machine guns, forward-firing rockets, and four 500-lb. anti-sub depth charges. For us torpedo pilots, the program was a welcome development, as anti-submarine duty would be more interesting than routine fleet patrols.

Hardly had we gotten started on ground schooling than orders came to break off training and go aboard ship—the USS *Altamaha* (CVE-18)—and be ready to sail within 36 hours. Planes had to be serviced and loaded abroad. We scrambled frantically. At dawn, March 30, we sailed, and after we were safely at sea, we got our combat orders from our skipper, Herb Bragg. It was an emergency anti-submarine hunter-killer mission. The location: "Mid-Pacific." The hasty nature of our orders gave us a hint that something out of the ordinary had been learned.

Steaming westward, we commenced anti-sub searches over the trackless ocean. It seemed like a fruitless mission: to comb the whole Pacific Ocean, with its millions of square miles and an endless panorama of waves and wind. But on the second day of searching, we had two contacts with submarines. Pilots Joe Polski and Charlie Edwards—one torpedo plane and one fighter, flying together—attacked one sub. Ensign Dwight and Lt. J. P. Fox hit another. After his attack, Polski, flying the torpedo plane, saw an oil slick and debris on the surface and excitedly called his radioman to get pictures. "We'll need them for proof of the hit. I'll circle." An hour later, back aboard ship, Polski and his radioman rushed the negatives down to the photo lab for development, while the rest of us waited breathlessly. Shortly, a photographer's mate came into the ready room with a long face. "There aren't any pictures" he said. "The lens cap was on the camera." After the war, a search of

Japanese naval records indicated that the sub had indeed been sunk April 4, 1944. A "kill" was credited to Polski and Edwards and their crews, but they had waited five years for confirmation.

After the war I also learned why we had such "luck" in finding and striking two Japanese submarines in one place at the same time in the middle of the vast Pacific. The U.S. had succeeded in breaking the Japanese code and had intercepted Japanese messages that our supply lines westward were in serious jeopardy. Our squadron, VC-66, was the spearhead of the counter-attack which limited the Japanese threat.

Run-in with an Admiral

From time to time after the war, I was asked if I had ever known "Admiral So-and-So." Though I count many admirals among my friends now, at the time of the war a young "j.g." (lieutenant junior grade) was not likely to know many admirals.

Yet an admiral and a j.g. sometimes did meet, and my first such contact was aboard the aircraft carrier *Fanshaw Bay* (CVE-70), bound for Manus Harbor in the Admiralty Islands, north of New Guinea in the Dutch East Indies. We were in Japanese-controlled water, so every morning we flew anti-submarine patrols. Our squadron had lost three TBF torpedo bombers, and we were down to a minimum number of planes required to fulfill our mission. We continued our search patrols forward of the fleet. As I completed the first of two legs, I detected a roughness in the engine. My engine kept running, but I decided to skip the last leg and head back to the carrier. I voice-radioed the ship for permission to come aboard in an emergency landing. After hearing my predicament, the air officer said, "Wait." As the task force flagship, we had several layers of command, and after a long pause, I heard the gruff voice of Adm. C. A. F. ("Ziggy") Sprague asking, "What's your problem?" I told him.

The task force consisted of two carriers with destroyer escorts, and—not expecting any of the planes back so soon—they were all steaming out of the wind. As I watched, I saw the DEs begin their turns, followed by the carriers, 180 degrees, putting them into the wind and in position to land my plane. Then came the admiral's voice again: "OK, make your approach; we'll bring you aboard."

I dropped down to 500 feet, flew the customary parallel course, and prayed that my engine would keep running, through the final approach, up the groove. I got the cut, caught a wire, and cut the throttle. I told the plane captain to take the aircraft below and find out what was wrong with the engine. I went back to the ready room to stand by until we got a report from the engineering department.

Finally, a message came from the bridge. The admiral wanted to see me. I climbed the ladder and saluted Captain Johnson, the skipper of the carrier. He pointed to Admiral Sprague, who started right in.

"Lieutenant."

"Yes, sir."

"Lieutenant," he said again. "We sent your plane down for an inspection by engineering, and they didn't find anything wrong with it."

Oh, My Lord, I was in trouble.

He said, "Lieutenant, do you know what you have done? We are in enemy waters, and you turned this whole fleet around. What do you have to say about that?"

I was temporarily silenced, but I began thinking fast.

"Admiral," I said, "I'm sorry to have caused this inconvenience, but I didn't turn this fleet around. I only asked permission to come aboard. *You* turned the fleet around."

Silence. He glared at me, and I waited for his reply. I could almost hear the admiral thinking, *"My God, he's right."*

"That'll be all," he said. And that was the end of that. I had two other conservations with Admiral Sprague that were much more congenial. Steaming into waters around Halmahera Island, in the Molucca Islands of the Dutch East Indies, where the Japanese were still in control, we were alerted by Air Combat Intelligence office (ACI) that the Japanese might shadow us with some of our captured American planes, PBYs, that would look like our own forces.

On a morning patrol, I caught sight of a PBY flying eastward from Japanese- controlled Galela Bay, which was surrounded by Halmahera. It looked innocent, flying at about 2,000 feet, but it was heading toward our task force, and it could give away our position if it was being flown by Japanese. But was it? I sent blinker messages with the identification signal of the day, but I got no response. Should I shoot him down? There was the possibility the he might be one of our own.

I decided to break radio silence and call for advice. Again, the gruff voice of Admiral Sprague asking what was wrong. I explained the quandary and the admiral didn't hesitate. "Fly down alongside," he said. "Look in the window and see if the bastard has slant eyes." Those were my orders. I alerted Joe Fernandez, my turret gunner, and "Swede" Swenson, my radio-man tail gunner. I did a sharp wing-over and down we went, guns trained on the PBY. As we crept up on his stern we gave him another recognition signal by my blinker. Still no response. With guns at the ready, I pulled alongside and looked in his cockpit window to "see if he had slant eyes." No, not at all. He was a happy-go-lucky American waving jauntily, without the slightest idea that he had almost been shot out of the sky. He was just flying fat, dumb and happy, having not bothered to answer my blinker challenge with the recognition signal of the day.

Air Cover on Morotai

Admiral Sprague gave me one more incident to remember him by. As the *Fanshaw Bay* steamed into the waters around the island of Morotai, we were guarding against Japanese attacks from the air. The most vulnerable time was at dawn, when Japanese raiders could fly from the Celebes to the west. After our troop ships had moved into the harbor of Morotai, preparing for land attacks, the Japanese would fly at high altitudes and drop their bombs, so our gunners were on alert. To protect against these raids, the Army general in command had asked Admiral Sprague to provide air cover at dawn and dusk. My assignment was to take three TBFs and cover for transports in the harbor against bombing.

It was September 15, 1944. Army troops from the 31st infantry division were going ashore on Morotai, to seize the island from the Japanese and establish a major base for retaking the Philippines and continuing to edge towards Japan. Gen. Douglas MacArthur was wading ashore with the second assault. I was leading a V-formation of TBFs at 12,000 feet to give them air cover. Suddenly my gunner called me on the intercom to say he was spotting puffs of black smoke coming up at us. It was anti-aircraft fire, but it was coming from *our* ships—they were firing at us! I decided not to wait for the Army gunners to realize their mistake. I ordered my two TBF wingmen to execute that well-known Naval maneuver known as "getting the hell out of there." We did. And back aboard ship, I reported the incident to Admiral Sprague. The admiral called his Army opposite to complain. He told the general: "I don't know whether to be mad as hell at you for shooting at us, or scared as hell that you couldn't hit us."

Near Misses

Early in my training at Pensacola in the fall of 1942, some of my friends—good young candidates for Naval air service—crashed and were killed before ever seeing the enemy. There was Fielding Mercer from Winnetka, Illinois. "Fee" Mercer would have made a fine Naval officer, but flying over Pensacola Bay, in an old pre-war P2V, an engine failed and he crashed. The same thing happened to Alan Gottlieb. And my friend Ben Davis let his Piper Cub get slow as he was tracking torpedoes. He stalled and went straight down into the water.

We all knew that we could be next, but we hoped there would only be close calls. I had some close calls of my own. During one carrier landing practice on a field at Pensacola (a "bounce drill"), my plane was an out-of-date scout called the OS2U, with which we could fly in and out of improvised landing fields surrounded by pine forests. On one such pass, I touched down on the tarmac and poured on the coal for take-off, but somehow couldn't get altitude. The trees were coming fast and I still couldn't get above them. The engine seemed sluggish and I was sure I was going to crash, when I quickly realized what was wrong. I had put the propeller in low pitch for the let-down, but I hadn't put it back in high pitch for take-off. So with seconds to go, I shoved the propeller-pitch button full forward and at the last second picked up enough power to clear the trees. It was just one of those near misses that we all had—if we were lucky.

The Puget Sound area of Washington provided its full share. With fog over the Sound and mountains on all sides, Seattle is a wonderful place for learning to deal with weather. Flying from an auxiliary air station in Shelton, Washington one day on the Olympic Peninsula, I encountered fog at 100 feet off the water. With another plane flying close on my wing, we suddenly lost visibility and had nothing to guide on. I had to hold a steady course, praying that my wingman would too. I radioed him to climb left, make a 180-degree turn and fly back into clear air. I would fly straight-ahead and climb out of it. I was sure it wouldn't take long to reach clear air. But I climbed, and climbed, and climbed, up to 5,000 feet. Still no visibility. I hoped there was no mountain ahead. I set a northerly heading, knowing that Mt. Rainier, Mt. Hood and Mount St. Helens were all to the east. At 10,000 feet I finally broke out into the sun. And there were the mountain ranges, but I still had to get down. So I began a slow descent. When I reached 2,000 feet I still had no visibility. I gingerly let down some more. Altimeters are sometimes wrong, but I let down some more—to 1,000 feet, 700, 600 and a final descent to 500 feet. There...finally clear! Gingerly—just skimming the waves—I sneaked my way back home. My wingman, Lt. Bob Weaver, was already there and said, "Where the hell were you? I've been back for half an hour!" Just another close call.

One of the most exotic forms of near misses is to almost get shot down by one of your own ships. It happened to me in the Marshall Islands where the old battleship USS *Washington* was bombarding Japanese positions on Wotje Atoll. On the shore were gun emplacements so thick that ordinary bombing by aircraft had not been able to dislodge them. Battleships were called upon for one of their last missions of the war, as they could fire, from a great distance away, 16-inch projectiles that might penetrate the underground chambers of the Japanese emplacements.

Battleship float planes would be shot out of the air by the Japanese, so a call came to the captain of the USS *Nassau* for help in spotting for the battleship gunners. The skipper cast his eyes around the ready room and his eyes lit on me. "Kip, how about it? Do you want to do some spotting for a battleship?"

I didn't know anything about spotting for a battleship. I didn't know about trajectory or range or ballistics of battleship projectiles. I only knew that they were 16- inches long and made a helluva blast when they hit. But I said I was game to try.

I was supposed to circle the target and report how the previous volley of shells had hit—short, long, right, left—and by how much. Arriving over Wotje, I stationed myself where I could view the Japanese positions, cruising at about 6,000 feet. Suddenly my radioman, "Swede" Swenson, called on the intercom: "Sir, there's something that looks like a flight of hornets coming right at us." Then...whoosh...there they went, a few hundred feet to starboard. I saw the same thing—big black blurs streaking past our wing. Except they weren't hornets. They were 16-inch shells from the battleship *Washington*, intended for the Japanese. They went up to 6,000 feet before they started to head back to earth. And they almost got us. No one had told me that battleship shells reached such heights. I decided that 10,000 feet would be more comfortable. And it was.

Rescue on Wasile Bay

To protect our land forces on Morotai west of New Guinea, Squadron VC-66 was ordered to neutralize enemy forces on the island of Halmahera.

As General MacArthur's Army Air Corps had no operating airfields in the region, Admiral Nimitz had agreed to assign him the Seventh Fleet under Adm. Thomas C. Kincaid, to be his forward air force and give him air cover while his troops were going ashore in the island-hopping approach to the Philippines. As part of the Seventh Fleet, our ship, the *Fanshaw Bay,* was the designated flag ship for our disposition.

On the second day of the Morotai assault, Sept. 16, our squadron was ordered to attack a Japanese airfield at Galela Bay off Halmahera Island, to keep the Japanese planes on the ground and protect our landing forces. In this we had the assistance of another squadron of fighters and torpedo bombers from a second carrier in the task force. During the morning hours I remained in the ready room as the first half of our torpedo pilots made strafing and bombing runs on the field. In the afternoon, we took our turn to finish the job. Over Galela Bay, which was surrounded by the Island of Halmahera, the anti-aircraft fire was continuous but scattered.

While we were thus engaged we got radio reports to stay on station for a follow-up assignment. It seemed that a fighter pilot from our neighboring carrier was down in the waters of Wasile Bay, between Halmahera and Morotai. He was wounded, but a Catalina rescue plane had dropped him a rubber raft, which he was able to tie to the anchor chain of an unmanned Japanese cargo ship just 200 yards from the enemy-occupied beach. His squadron mates circled overhead, strafing the Japanese position to prevent them from trying to capture our pilot, but they were running out of fuel and had to go back to their carrier. Another Catalina pontoon plane tried to land and rescue him, but it was driven off by intense anti-aircraft fire. That's when our squadron was called in to keep holding the Japanese at bay, strafing the shoreline and dropping bombs if necessary— anything to prevent enemy vessels from getting to our pilot.

How our fellow was to be rescued we didn't know until another instruction came from the ship: Two PT boats were on their way to get him. They were approaching the mouth of the harbor, and we should be careful not to strafe in the area in which they were running. We continued to circle. One of our torpedo pilots, Lt. Al Mayer, was laying smoke along the beach to screen the action in the bay.

We continued to circle. We had about four hours of fuel, and only two hours had transpired, so we waited to give air cover during the PT boats' final dash into the bay. Finally one of the PT boats started its move towards the downed pilot, under heavy fire at close range. From our altitude, the only thing visible was a thin wake of white water and a little sliver at the tip. The PT boat stopped dead in the water and splashes of foam rose around it, as the Japanese shore batteries fired away. Then another spurt of white water, and the boat was heading toward the exit from the bay.

At this point, we were ordered to return to ship, and I didn't know what happened after that. But I did think, at the time, that whoever that guy was down there on that PT boat had done a hulluva job. He put himself in harm's way. He was cool, and I hope he had rescued the downed pilot and they had got back all right. Whoever he was, he deserved some real praise for that job. We appreciated guys like him.

It was many years later, in 1968, that I found out what had happened that day in Wasile Bay—when I read the obituary of a business acquaintance of mine, A. Murray Preston, vice president of the American Security and Trust Company, a Washington, D.C. bank. I learned that Preston was the lieutenant who skippered that PT boat, and he had received the Medal of Honor for his bravery. I had known him for 20 years, but I never knew that he was the man on the surface of the water when my fellow pilots and I were up there giving him air protection. It led me to think that all of us should write our own obituaries and publish them while we are still living.

The War Is Over

"This is the way the world ends, not with a bang but a whimper." When T. S. Eliot wrote those words, he obviously did not have in mind the end of a global conflict like World War II. Yet, to a few young warriors, including some of the pilots in my Navy squadron, the end of the war conjured up some bewildering thoughts. What would we do now? For three or four years, we had focused on one goal—victory in war, flying military airplanes, taking off and landing aboard ships in the middle of the sea, dropping bombs and strafing and avoiding being shot down by other ships and planes and ground fire. There were thoughts of home, but as time went on, it seemed increasingly unlikely that we would get there. Then it became a reality.

I heard the news in a flash report while flying back from Seattle to Pasco, Washington. As flight leader of my new unit, Torpedo Squadron 23, I had my headset turned to the military frequency. Suddenly my wingman started jinking wildly, wagging his wings and pointing to his earphones and waving his arms. I thought he had gone crazy—until it struck me that he was trying to get me to listen to something on the radio. I turned to a news report. Japan had surrendered! It was August 14, 1945, and the war was over.

Wild celebrations erupted across the United States. That night the pilots of VT 23 went for a picnic on the banks of the Snake River where it flows into the Columbia. Unlike the exuberant crowds in Times Square, ours was a somber gathering—for the men, at any rate. The wives and girlfriends were ecstatically happy. Their men were safe and things would turn out all right. The men weren't so sure. They had been prepared for the final act—the big show, the invasion of Japan. Now, blessedly, that was not needed—but *they* were not needed either. The war was over, but what next?

One of those ecstatically happy wives at our picnic on the Snake River was mine—Mary Louise ("Gogo") Cobb Kiplinger. We had married eight months earlier, after a courtship that started in Ft. Lauderdale, Fla., when I was stationed at the Naval air station there in February of '43 and she was vacationing with her parents. It continued in April, when I was sent for carrier training on Lake Michigan to Glenview field, near Chicago and very near Gogo's hometown of Winnetka, Ill. Through we had just a few weeks together over the span of almost two years, we had maintained an active correspondence while I was at sea, culminating in a brief engagement when my squadron returned to the states. Within a few days of our wedding in Winnetka on Dec. 11, 1944, my bride and I arrived in Jacksonville, Fla., for my next Navy assignment. I never went to sea again, and we spent the months before VJ Day at bases in Florida, California and Washington State. By the end of the war, Gogo was pregnant; our first son, Todd, would be born in November of 1945.

Now, after spending four years at war, I was a husband and father-to-be, and before long I would once again be a civilian. It was time to consider the next phase of my life.

8

A New Kind of Magazine

The war was over. Twelve million young men and women were returning to civilian life. My father, whose Kiplinger Letters for business managers had become very successful during the New Deal and World War II, was hatching a new editorial idea: a magazine of practical economics.

It would counsel its readers—mostly businessmen at first—not just on issues facing their enterprises, but also on how to deal with the whole range of perplexing financial questions in their personal lives: homeownership, insurance, cars, saving for their futures, maybe even investing in sophisticated things like stocks (which very few households owned in 1945).

For most of his life, W. M. Kiplinger had written on economic subjects like government regulations, interest rates, markets, foreign trade, inflation and profits. But similar subjects, reported from a different angle, he reasoned, were of interest to everyone in their personal lives. They had jobs, they had to pay bills, borrow money, figure interest and plan ahead. Why not publish something for these concerns, too?

My father had started writing to me about his idea in early 1945, and he suggested that I join him in the venture after the war. I was still in the Navy, with no idea of how long the conflict might last. I had thought some about going back into newspaper journalism after the war, perhaps in Chicago, my wife's home city. But I accepted my father's offer to return to Washington when the war was over, to help him start a new magazine.

My father and I had worked together on *The Kiplinger Washington Letter* and in writing the book *Washington is Like That* (which, when published in 1942, became a national best-seller). We meshed well, and he would be, of course, the "Senior Officer Present," which my Navy experience had taught me to respect. I had no doubt that things would go well.

The war ended in August, 1945, and in October I was released from active duty. By December, Gogo and I and our new-born son, Todd, were in Washington, and I was ready to report for new duty in civilian life as executive editor of a magazine that didn't yet exist. I bought a small brick house on Willard Avenue in the quiet Friendship Heights neighborhood of Chevy Chase, Md., right across the District line. It cost $12,000, which I financed with my wartime savings and a $10,000 mortgage at 4¼%, payable quarterly, interest only.

The New Staff

For the first few weeks, I worked out of the Kiplinger Letter offices in the National Press Building—on the same 11th floor where I had worked as an office boy in 1935, a junior reporter in 1939 and an editorial assistant on the Washington book in 1941. It was familiar but it was cramped; clearly we needed another location.

I located a small second-floor space—someone's former apartment—in a brick building on 14th Street, a block above Thomas Circle. The front room would serve as an editorial bullpen, and the back bedroom would be my office. Downstairs was a typewriter repair shop, and through the wall to the north, a fortuneteller. (Editorial wags suggested that we poke a hole through the wall and join forces with the psychic seer.) Not long thereafter, we outgrew that space and moved our offices to an historic townhouse in a better neighborhood near the White House, at 1729 G Street, N.W.

The staff, which I gradually assembled during 1946, was a motley but talented group of seasoned journalists from all over the country, all starting out on a new phase in their career. The new managing editor (ME) was John Denson, a veteran newspaperman and recently an associate editor of *Fortune* magazine in New York. His assistant ME, John W. (Jack) Randolph, had been a newspaperman in Washington and New York. Senior Editor Clarence G. Marshall had been managing editor of David Lawrence's *U. S. News* magazine in Washington. Diana Hirsh had been national affairs editor at *Newsweek*. Thomas Drake (Tom) Durrance had been a Washington and war correspondent for *TIME* magazine. Maurice English had been a foreign correspondent for the *Chicago Tribune*. Scott Hart (who occupied the third-floor semi-attic in the G Street townhouse) had worked for newspapers in Washington and Richmond and had been a contributing editor at *Esquire* and *Coronet* magazines. Joe Slevin had taught at the universities of Nebraska and Illinois but, after Navy service, was aiming for a career in economic journalism.

Others of our new writing and editing staff had worked at the *Wall Street Journal*, Cincinnati *Enquirer*, Baltimore *Sun*, *PM* magazine in New York, Canadian papers, the *Oregon Journal*, Washington *Daily News*, Providence *Journal* and *Editorial Research Reports*.

Meeting together in our first offices on 14th Street, we deciphered and digested a memorandum from W. M. Kiplinger on the idea behind this new magazine. It seemed clear to him, but it didn't fit any standard publishing category. There were magazines "of general interest," like the newsweeklies, *LIFE* and *Saturday Evening Post*. There were business and financial publications. There were industrial trade publications. There were magazines for women and for men. But a magazine of "consumer interest" or "consumer economics"? Those words were not in the publishing lexicon at that time. There was the non-profit *Consumer Reports,* of course, but that was a product-testing magazine. There were no periodicals that aimed to help business people and families with what came to be called their "personal finances."

The Mission of the Magazine

In fact, W. M. Kiplinger didn't have a neat description for his magazine either, although his editorial memorandum of March, 1946, included a list of topics to be covered. It listed such prospective articles and topics as "Pick the Job that Fits You," "How to Treat Your Congressman," "Mansions for $5,000," "Foreign Trade for Small Businesses," "The Job Outlook," "One Man's Formula for Painless Exercise," "Stock Market Comments," "Price Trends," "Off-Season Vacations," "The Ready-Made Kitchen Industry,"

"International Exchange of Students," and "The 36-Hour Week." And he wanted "plenty of stuff for housewives, but not labeled as such."

At the end of his topics list, he added this caveat: "There is no fixed and frozen policy. The policy will be a fluid thing." That postscript may have been the most prophetic statement in the whole memorandum. The first year of publication, 1947, proved to be a stormy shake-down cruise, with the new staff struggling to find the right voice, mission and mix of stories for the new magazine, which had been named *Kiplinger Magazine* and subtitled *The Changing Times*. The editor in chief, W. M. Kiplinger, was a tough boss who rarely seemed satisfied with what the new staff was producing.

In the first two years, 1946 and '47, the magazine had a lot of features and advice stories for people who owned and managed businesses—who, after all, were the core readers of the Kiplinger Letters and the subscriber base from which the new magazine was launched.

In the introduction to the first issue, in January of 1947, W. M. Kiplinger pointed out that this was not a "news magazine." "It is," he said, "mainly for businessmen, but businessmen have broad interests and human interests, so the scope of this magazine will be both broad and human."

Besides the novelty of its subject matter, the magazine was unusual as a business venture, too. It carried no advertising, to ensure its independence from outside commercial pressure. It would be sold by subscription only, not available on newsstands. And it was pricey—$6 for 12 monthly issues, the equivalent of about $60 in

2011 dollars. It was published in a small format on uncoated paper, with no photographs and few illustrations. Articles were leanly written and brief —mostly one page. And there were no writer's bylines—an alien concept in magazine journalism.

The magazine would contain a lot of the forecasts that were the stock-in-trade of the Kiplinger Letters. In a department called "The Year Ahead," the first issue proclaimed that 1947 would be "the most trying year since the end of the war. American blood will be spilled abroad—in Palestine or Greece or Turkey, for American troops will form a great part of UN forces. Russia will gain the first half of the year, and recede in the second half. War fears will rise, but there probably will be no war. The Marshall Plan will be pushed with a new grimness. In the U.S., Republicans will have the edge in elections. Unions will get a third round of wage boosts. Prices will go on rising until late in the year. The recession could come in late '48, but probably will be delayed until '49. The year will be full of dangers."

The second issue had some guidance for employers about handling alcoholism in the workplace, and it admonished readers to be sure to put their wills and life insurance in order. By April, 1947, we were writing about "our challenging national medical problem." We all moaned about "the high cost of coffee" (50 cents a pound) and "the oil shortage." A year later, in January, 1948, we led off with articles on household gadgets, shoplifting and standardized dress sizes.

Gradually through the first year, the table of contents showed more and more articles about personal finances and the household:

"34 million housewives," summer family touring, small cars, preparing your income tax return, and "Plan Your Estate Now."

In June, we wrote about gasoline shortages and what a young couple should do to live on $3,400 a year. In that same month came the lodestar piece: "What a Young Man Should Do With His Money—If Any," written by John W. (Jack) Hazard, who later became senior editor of the magazine. The article contained advice from four different sources: an investment counselor, an estate lawyer, a stock broker and an insurance agent.

What did they tell the young man? The investment counselor advised him to save $50 a month until he got $2,000, then buy a $20,000 life insurance policy, some savings bonds and eventually a home. After all that, he should start buying stocks on a regular basis.

The estate lawyer put life insurance first, then an emergency fund consisting of bonds. After this the young man should buy into his own company stock or invest in a building and loan association.

The broker went at it right up front: "Buy good stocks."

The life insurance agent advised that 10% of the young man's income should go into life insurance immediately, split between term and permanent insurance. The rest, he said, should go into savings bonds. And he added, "Don't rush into stocks or a house until you have plenty of cash."

We never knew how readers followed the scenarios, but the article set a course for the magazine, which grew and matured into the first pure "personal finance magazine." In the first three years the stories about small-business management gradually left the magazine, and in 1949, the title and subtitle were reversed. It became *Changing Times*, the Kiplinger Magazine.

It would be another 25 years later before the second magazine of personal-finance guidance, *Money* from Time, Inc., was launched in the fall of 1972, patterned closely after our *Changing Times* (but containing pages of advertising, which wouldn't appear in our magazine until 1980).

The Dewey Debacle

The most difficult episode in the early life of *Kiplinger Magazine* was its handling of the presidential campaign of 1948, between Democratic incumbent Harry S Truman and his Republican challenger, Thomas E. Dewey. Dewey had made his reputation as a prosecuting attorney crusading against the crime syndicate in New York. The Truman administration was plagued by the "10 percenter" scandals, cronyism and a general disarray in the congressional legislative program.

As the campaign progressed, my father became increasingly convinced that Truman would be replaced by Dewey as President. In his weekly Letters, he tracked the odds, which were then overwhelmingly against Truman. Even our Democratic sources at the White House were convinced that "the jig was up," and—one by one—they began casting around for new jobs. My father's Letters just before the election predicted not only a Dewey victory, but his reelection in 1952!

As editor in chief of the new magazine, my father decided that this newcomer to the publishing world could make a big name for itself by publishing a "detailed and authoritative" account of what the new administration would advocate—a program on which Kiplinger readers could base their own plans, business and personal. So the entire November, 1948 issue would be devoted to this subject, with a cover that proclaimed, "What Dewey Will Do." There was considerable opposition to this risky plan from several senior editors of both the Letters and magazine, but W. M. Kiplinger brushed it off and the plan went forward.

Some of the subjects were covered by the magazine's own staff, some were based on the reporting by the weekly Letter staff. We had to close our issue six weeks ahead of the election in order to get the issue copy-edited, designed, type-set, printed and into the mail for November reading, so much of the substantive reporting was two months old on election day. At the time we were closing the issue, public opinion polls were still showing Dewey leading Truman by a wide margin, and most of our editorial staff was confident that Truman was on his way out.

The 30,000 copies of the Dewey issue were already on press a few days before the election, to ensure that they could be mailed immediately after balloting on Tuesday, Nov. 2. But the day before, Monday, W. M. Kiplinger made a fateful decision to mail half of the copies immediately. We would score a big coup, as the first publication to explain in detail what the Dewey administration would do and how it would affect the readers' interests. (An ad for copies of the special Kiplinger issue was even ordered to be placed in the election week issue of *TIME* magazine.) But some of the staff was very nervous.

Then came election day. My father left the office early and went home to prepare for a celebratory dinner party that he and his wife, LaVerne, were hosting that evening with some friends at their home in Bethesda. I went to the National Press Club to watch election results on the ticker. As the evening wore on, strange numbers began appearing on the broadband ticker on a screen across the end of the main lounge. In state by state, the numbers showed Truman was leading. "Incredible," I thought. Still they came. My colleague Jack Hazard and I conferred. This was a shock, but we had to call my father to tell him, and we did. He was startled, but still not certain that the final results wouldn't show Dewey the victor the next morning. They didn't.

A greater professional blow none of us had ever felt. Our reportorial and editorial objectivity had been put on the line and we failed. We had been proven wrong. It did not help that nearly everyone else was wrong too, because we were not supposed to follow everyone. We were supposed to be right.

W. M. Kiplinger swallowed hard, but decided to acknowledge our error forthrightly—and mail the rest of the November issues to our readers, as promised. It was a bitter pill to swallow, but swallow it we did. The magazine's next issue featured articles on how to deal with the new Democratic administration in the White House and in Congress—labor influence, taxes, credit, living costs, rental rates and Christmas retail sales.

Changing Leadership

There was a lot of tension and staff turnover during those first two years of the magazine, as we experimented and tinkered to get things right. Managing Editor Denson left early in the game—in April of '47—and I took over his duties. We all knew that the magazine start-up would be costly, but it turned out to be a bigger financial burden than expected, and it was cutting deep into the profitability of the whole company—and its long tradition of generous profit-sharing. The Dewey mess just exacerbated the stress around the office.

Most of the editors and writers of that first staff in 1947 gradually left, and many of them distinguished themselves in their later jobs. Denson became editor of *Newsweek* in 1953 and editor in chief of the New York *Herald Tribune* in the 1960s. Diana Hirsh became an editor at *Colliers*, a researcher and writer for former President Herbert Hoover, and a campaign speech writer for John F. Kennedy and Robert F. Kennedy in the 1950s and '60s. In 1954 Maurice English founded *Chicago*, a pioneering city magazine. Scott Hart wrote a highly regarded Civil War history book published in 1949, *Eight April Days*, the story of the fighting that led up to Robert E. Lee's surrender at Appomattox. Joe Slevin became a prominent economic journalist, writing a widely syndicated newspaper column and publishing his own newsletter, *The Washington Bond Report.* Tom Durrance left to get a federal government job, which served as grist for an electrifying 1954 article in the *Saturday Evening Post,* "I Road Uncle Sam's Gravy Train," about living a life of high pay and lavish perks as a foreign affairs aide at a federal agency in

Washington. Jack Randolph went on to become the outdoors editor of the *New York Times*.

As impressive as our *Kiplinger Magazine* "alumni club" turned out to be, several very talented writers and editors on that first staff stayed at Kiplinger for years. Herbert L. Brown, Jr., who had been an editorial writer at the Cincinnati *Enquirer*, rose to the top editor's job, guiding the young magazine firmly into its personal-finance mission. Reg Ingraham, a former AP correspondent and Rome bureau chief for *TIME*, moved over to the staff of *The Kiplinger Washington Letter* and became a mainstay of that publication. Jack Hazard, a former *Wall Street Journal* reporter who was my first hire for our new magazine in 1946, became Kiplinger's chief investment writer and one of the top financial journalists in America. Jack also authored several best-selling Kiplinger books on investing strategies.

In mid-1948, well before the Dewey debacle, I had decided to leave the Kiplinger organization and seek a journalism job elsewhere, probably in Chicago. The magazine launch had been an exhilarating challenge for me as a young editor in my late 20s, but it put quite a strain on my relationship with my father, personally and professionally. I thought that a break would do us both a lot of good.

9

Chicago! Chicago!

In November, 1948, with President Truman's upset of Dewey rocking the political world, I was on my way to Chicago to find my next journalistic challenge. With my wife, Gogo, and two small sons in tow (our second, Knight, had been born in February), we rolled into the Windy City.

I had decided to hit the *Chicago Daily News,* Col. Frank Knox's estimable afternoon newspaper, for a job as a business reporter. I went to see the business editor and I told him of my earlier work on the *Ithaca Journal, San Francisco Chronicle, Kiplinger Washington Letter* and *Kiplinger Magazine.* He was friendly but he didn't have any place open.

Before making my next call, I went to see Merrill Meigs, vice president of the Hearst Corporation and a former publisher of Hearst's two Chicago dailies, the morning *Herald & Examiner* and *Evening American.* (He was also a golfing friend of my father-in-law, E. P. ["Ev"] Cobb, who was an executive of the Morgan Linen Service, a Chicago-based national firm that supplied tablecloths and napkins to hotels, railroads and restaurants.) "Mr. Meigs," I asked, "if you were a young man in my position looking for a job as a business writer, where would you go?" Without hesitation, he said, "I wouldn't. There's no money in it."

Well, he was right, but that was what I wanted to do, so I went on to see Col. John D. Ames, editor and publisher of the *Chicago Journal of Commerce*, who had sold the paper to the Ridder brothers (of the *New York Journal of Commerce*) the year before but stayed on to run it. After some back-and-forthing about my experience, he asked, "How would you like to write a column?" I hadn't ever written a daily column, but I agreed to take a shot at it. Then he asked how much I wanted to get paid. I said I'd been getting $12,000 a year, to which he responded: "I don't deal in 'thousands a year.' I'll pay you $140 a week." After some fast mental calculation, I realized that I would be taking a big cut in pay, but I said yes.

Settling into Chicago

A few weeks later, on my first day of work, I checked in with Ames, who made me feel welcome but also took the opportunity to remind me I was not the editorial voice of the paper. That role was to remain with Wilbur Brons, my predecessor as author of the column, "The Round Table." He was still director of the editorial pages. I was to be a separate voice—"informative, entertaining, independent." But I was not to be so independent that I would insult anybody the paper wanted as a friend. As I was leaving John Ames' office he asked me where I was staying. I told him The Croydon. He gasped and said, "Do you know about that place?" "Well," I said, "It looked clean and pleasant, but I noticed that it seemed to have a lot of fancily dressed women sitting around the lobby."

"That," he said, "is because the hotel is owned by the Mafia, and that's where they keep their molls." I moved out the next day. I eventually found a home for my family in the quiet suburb of Northfield, on Chicago's North Shore west of Winnetka, Gogo's hometown. It was a newish "ranch house" (one-story) on Eaton Street, a dead-end block with lots of young families like ours. All the couples socialized, and the sidewalks were full of kids on tricycles.

I began to like this new invigorating place called Chicago. Having worked in the tree-shaded, monumental city of Washington, I now rode the train to the *Journal of Commerce*'s offices on Grand Avenue, north of the Chicago River, and I looked into the windows of apartments along the way. In San Francisco, where I had worked before the war, I had been able to see the bay, smell the salt air and struggle up and down steep hills. In Chicago, there were no hills, and the wind came from any direction. By my nose, I could appraise the weather. If it was from the east, it carried the fresh smell of Lake Michigan. If it blew from the north, it came past Dr. Scholl's corn-plaster plant, with its unmistakable aroma of foot balm. From the west, the wind carried fumes from the Morton Salt plant and the railroad yards west of The Loop. A west-southwest wind brought smells of General Motors' Electro-Motive plant, which manufactured diesel railroad engines. A southwest wind brought odors from the stockyards, and a south wind the aroma of steelmaking in South Chicago and Gary, Ind., and the oil refineries of Whiting, Ind. As I smelled my way to work, I could plan my day in accordance with the weather.

Giants of Business

For a young journalist barely 30 years old, it was an exciting experience being a columnist in Chicago. I met and interviewed many of the big names in American business: Gen. Robert E. Wood, chairman of Sears Roebuck; Sewell Avery, the mercurial head of Montgomery Ward; Fowler McCormick, Jr., boss of his family's International Harvester; and Edward Eagle Brown, chairman of the First National Bank of Chicago. All of them headed companies in the billion-dollar category at a time when a billion dollars was "real money." In addition to these gray eminences of Chicago business, I also got to know Chuck Percy, a boy wonder who became president of the Bell & Howell camera company at the age of 30 (probably the youngest CEO of a major U.S. company at the time) and would later serve three terms in the U.S. Senate.

As the front-page columnist for the *Chicago Journal of Commerce*, I had *carte blanche* to call on them and write about them. The only problem was that they regarded the paper as such a friend of business that, whenever I wrote anything critical or just objectively independent, they took umbrage. After one column I wrote about General Wood, he told me, "I didn't think you were going to write what I said."

Gen. Charles G. Dawes was the most peppery of all these titans of industry in Chicago. His resume might have been the most impressive in American public service of that era. He had been a World War I general, winner of the Nobel Peace Prize, vice president of the United States under Coolidge, U.S. comptroller of the currency, and U.S. ambassador to Great Britain. He was a major stockholder in Pure Oil, his family's natural gas and oil company, and was now—in his early 80s—chairman of City National Bank and Trust Company.

One day while I sat typing in my office at the paper, managing editor Gordon Ewen called and asked me if I had a jacket with me. *Peculiar question*, I thought, but I told him I did. He said, "I have an invitation from General Dawes to round up a couple of friends and come down to the bank for lunch. He's alone and he wants some company." (Ewen would later sign on as public relations chief of the Dawes family's Pure Oil.)

So off we went to the bank on lower LaSalle Street, across from the Chicago Board of Trade. There we were joined by Lowell Snorf, a young lawyer who worked as a lobbyist at the state capitol in Springfield. We were shown to the bank's boardroom—a cavernous, high-ceilinged place where four places were set for lunch. Chairman Dawes came in with a cane, and when Ewen presented his friend Lowell Snorf, the General leaned forward, cupped his hand over his ear, and asked him to repeat his name again. "Snorf," he said, "Lowell Snorf." General Dawes looked quizzical and finally leaned over to me and whispered, "That's funny, I keep thinking he's saying *Snorf.*"

The conversation at lunch revolved around politics and President Harry Truman. We started talking about Truman's new appointee, Director of the Budget Frank Pace, and the General asked me what I thought of him. I told him I thought he was a very smart man. "He's a fool!" shouted Dawes, and he glared at me. I managed to get out the question, "Why do you say that, General?" "Because," he said, "I saw his picture in the paper this morning, and he was smiling! No budget director should ever smile." That was the hard-shell attitude of Charles G. Dawes, who himself had been the first director of the Bureau of the Budget when it was established in the Harding administration.

I heard a similar voice from an officer of Swift & Co., the big meat packer whose offices were on the South Side, just outside the stockyards. Porter Jarvis was his name, and he was the company treasurer (and later, president and chairman). While I was interviewing him one day, a young executive from the company stuck his head inside the door and asked if Mr. Jarvis had made any decision on "that matter we talked about."

When the door closed I asked Mr. Jarvis if he wanted me to go outside so he could talk with the other visitor. "No," he said, "I'll get to that later."

"You know," he continued, "that fellow is just asking me to put another item in the budget for a big new expansion in facilities—something we have talked about before. We'll get around to it in due time."

And then Jarvis explained how he dealt with requests for big new expenditures. When the request first came in, he listened, promised to give it consideration, then put the papers in the bottom drawer of his big imposing desk. If the requester came in a second time, Jarvis moved them up to the next drawer. And if the man came in a third time, with an urgent look on his face, Jarvis would pull the papers out, put them on the top of his desk, and prepare for a serious and final decision. *That* was the Chicago hair-shirt approach to corporate budgeting.

At the *Journal of Commerce*, my mail brought unexpected surprises from names I didn't recognize. One letter arrived postmarked Duluth, Minnesota. The sender wrote that a recent column of mine—about working with your bank and letting your banker be a friend rather than an enemy—was all well and good, but he had a special problem. He was having a hard time convincing his banker to lend him working capital against an inventory of bean sprouts. The banker didn't consider bean sprouts as viable collateral. *Bean sprouts?* I thought, *in Duluth, Minnesota?*

The sender of the letter was a man named Jeno Paulucci, who was building a company that pioneered the marketing of canned (and later frozen) Chinese foods under the Chun King brand. He apparently worked things out with his local banker. He built up Chun King and sold it in 1966 for $63 million, then grew a new company, Jeno's Pizza Rolls, which he sold in 1985 for $135 million.

Fascinating Characters

While I had had some contact with Adlai Stevenson during his time as governor of Illinois, I had never met his wife, Ellen Borden Stevenson, a Chicago heiress and arts patron who divorced the governor in 1949, his first year in office. It seemed to have been an amicable parting. He was interested in law and public affairs, and she was interested in the arts (in her own special way). She liked to host artsy salons in her home, attended by Chicagoans from various fields, including my wife Gogo and me on a few occasions.

One of her special interests was *avant garde* poetry, and she was the principal angel of the trendy magazine *Poetry*. To entertain guests at her home one evening with a poetry reading, she invited Maxwell Bodenheim—a celebrated American poet and novelist of the '20s and '30s who was, by then—unbeknownst to her guests—a derelict bohemian living in New York's Greenwich Village. Gogo and I listened dutifully to his poetry, but if my life depended on it, I could not now tell you what any of it meant.

On another occasion at Mrs. Stevenson's home, the "noted Viennese psychiatrist, Dr. Karl Weischuler," explained his new and revolutionary approach to psychoanalysis. We were introduced to a distinguished looking, grey-haired gentleman dressed in a cut-away coat and wearing spats. I thought the costume was a bit stagey, but Gogo said that it probably represented Dr. Weischuler's professional style and spirit of individuality. His voice was soft, and for nearly half an hour he held us in thrall.

Then, while we all sat in admiring silence, our hostess stood up and delivered a bombshell: "Dr. Weischuler," she revealed, was none other than Joseph ("Yellow Kid") Weil—the legendary flim-flam artist and swindler of wealthy pigeons, then in his early 70s and earning his living demonstrating his con-man's skills at soirees like this one.

The distinguished (and colorful) personalities visiting Chicago were not all impersonators and poets. Among the recognizable names was Vincent Astor, scion of the wealthy New York family, who came during the 1956 political conventions to exhibit a metal automobile house trailer that he had invented. With a distinctive flair, he parked it in a garden of a mansion on North Astor Street in the

Gold Coast neighborhood, and proceeded to dispense refreshments, explain his bullet-shaped trailer, and engage in conversation with political figures, delegates from the hinterlands and some political junkies (like me).

On United Nations Day, which was observed in Chicago despite the isolationist views of Col. McCormick's *Chicago Tribune*, the city hosted many supporters of internationalism, including former Sen. Warren Austin of Vermont, recently named U.S. ambassador to the UN, and beloved gospel singer Mahalia Jackson, who had lived in Chicago since her teenage years. In keeping with her music, she exuded love and welcome to all people. If Jackson detected some standoffishness from one of the white male guests, she would take his hand in her warm brown ones, move it around a little and say, "See, the color doesn't rub off."

At the same United Nations observance, British actor Basil Rathbone told the young people who came from the diverse nationalities and cultures that made up Chicago—Italian, German, Polish, Irish, African-American—"Hold onto your parents' languages and customs, they will enrich your life." I'm not sure that they followed his advice.

Ideas for Columns

In my columns for the *Journal of Commerce*, I mixed local subjects in with national issues. My first column was based on a conversation I had overheard while I was still in Washington. It was between Marriner Eccles, chairman of the Federal Reserve Board, and Tom Saltz, proprietor of Lewis & Thomas Saltz, the haberdashers on G Street where I had bought my suits. The conversation was about inflation and federal price controls, and it took place while Mr. Eccles was buying a suit. The subject hit home with buyers and sellers alike, and it set a tone for me to discuss economic subjects in everyday language.

A few months later, I found myself staring blankly at my typewriter without an idea for anything to write. After stalling around and wiping soot off my piles of papers, I began roaming around the office in search of a bright idea. *The Journal of Commerce* had innumerable departments on everything in business: capital markets, stocks, bonds, railroads, scrap iron, steel, every segment of manufacturing, retailing, women's fashions, and agricultural commodities. The rural life was celebrated in Chicago by Everett Mitchell's "National Farm and Home Hour," a weekly variety broadcast nationally on NBC from Chicago radio studios at WENR and later WMAQ. Chicago was also home to the celebrated "grain pit" of the Chicago Board of Trade, where farm commodities were traded in a raucous atmosphere like the trading floor of the New York Stock Exchange.

This morning, I was sure I could come up with a fresh subject for my column, but I struggled, so I picked up my hat and went to lunch. My lunch companion that day was director of the Henry George Society, an economic reform group named after the iconoclastic 19th century American theorist who was an inspiration to both liberals and conservatives in his era.

I found the director to be a stimulating and provocative companion, and on this day he told me a fable to illustrate how he believed we should think about economic subjects. Everything in economics, he said, is a matter of give-and-take, value-for-value-received, a simple exchange of goods and services. Every benefit also has a cost. In sum, he said, "there is no such thing as a free lunch."

I went back to the office thinking about that, and suddenly an idea struck me for the column. I set a scene in a mythical Middle Eastern country, where a young shah determined to teach his subjects all they needed to know about economics. He called in his wisest scholars and ordered them to produce a program to teach his people economics. Three months later, they returned with 16 volumes of illuminated manuscripts explaining in minute detail what they thought the people needed to know about economics (with charts, graphs and overlays). The young shah was impressed and started to award his scholars with his highest honor. Suddenly, his trusted eldest adviser, the grand vizier, held up his hand and said, "Stop! These men are imposters. I can tell you all you need to know about economics in just nine words." Taken aback, the young shah said, "If you can, I will give you the hand of the most beautiful girl in my harem. If you don't, you will be beheaded." With that, the grand vizier confidently proclaimed—impressing the shah and winning the girl—"There is no such thing as a free lunch!"

I wrote the piece and the column appeared the next morning. For weeks at the *Journal of Commerce*, the switchboard and my mail were flooded with requests for copies of that column. I couldn't go anywhere without being asked to tell the story. And many years later, in Washington, I had the pleasure of repeating it to Paul McCracken, chairman of the White House Council of Economic Advisors under President Richard Nixon.

Business reporters and columnists are accustomed to being challenged with hostility, depending on readers' points of view, but in Chicago in the 1950s, the atmosphere was open and free-wheeling. Still, I was not prepared for the degree of trust and goodwill I encountered from U.S. Treasury official Randolph Burgess, whom I interviewed as a broadcast journalist in 1953, when he came to Chicago to address a gathering of bankers. I cornered Mr. Burgess after his speech and began bombarding him with additional questions on monetary policy. After a couple of questions, he interrupted me and said: "I've got a plane to catch. You know what I think about all this. You make up a quote and attribute it to me. That'll be fine. Goodbye." Well, Mr. Burgess went back to Washington and I did make up an appropriate quote, and I never got a complaint from Randolph Burgess.

Big Ideas in Chicago

Covering business from Chicago was different from writing about economic policy in Washington. I was dealing with business action itself, where the rubber meets the road. This was about railroads, steel, oil, meatpacking, wheat, corn and soybeans, electronics, engines, beer and banking. It was lumber, shipping, insuring, wholesaling, and retailing, stocks, bonds and real estate.

Businessmen there believed in words of Chicago architect and planner Daniel Burnham, who proclaimed, "Make no little plans; they have no magic to stir men's blood." I encountered that spirit everywhere. It inspired a prominent local developer, Arthur Rubloff. He had bought city properties during the post-World War II building boom and had done quite well, but he had something more dramatic in mind. He conceived of a new luxury retail and office district along North Michigan Avenue, lying north of the Chicago River—past the Chicago Tribune Building, the Wrigley Building and the historic Chicago Water Tower, past the past the Palmolive Building (with its Lindbergh Beacon on top), all the way to the Drake Hotel.

I first heard about this grand scheme on a gray winter day. I had a call from Arthur Rubloff. He invited me to lunch, and we met at the Imperial House off Michigan Avenue. It was the first time I had met Arthur Rubloff (and the first time I had ever heard of a Caesar salad). He described his plan with great enthusiasm, calling it "The Magnificent Mile," and said it would someday supplant the downtown State Street district as the most prestigious shopping area in Chicago. I thought it was a crazy pipe dream. But he and other developers built it over many years, and Rubloff's vision was realized. Now there are similar luxury retail districts all around the world, from Minneapolis and Los Angeles to Hong Kong, Dubai and Singapore. (Some of them ape the Chicago original by calling themselves "The Miracle Mile.")

Chicago in the 1950s lived with the title of "Second City"— second to New York. Chicagoans themselves took every opportunity to travel to New York for theater and even for business that could have just as easily been transacted at home in the Windy City itself. New York was a good excuse for some fun. Fairfax ("Fax") Cone—a partner of the advertising agency Foote, Cone & Belding (successor to Albert Lasker's legendary Lord & Thomas agency in Chicago)—had a set of sumptuous offices on the top of 333 North Michigan Avenue, a landmark in its day. (In Chicago parlance at the time, "333" was code for prestigious advertising and public relations.) Yet many of Fax Cone's Chicago clients loved to travel to the agency's New York office (headed by partner Emerson Foote), where they could spend a couple of evenings at restaurants and theaters and charge the trip off as a business expense.

All the same, I—a lifelong easterner—found the Midwest a stimulating environment. And I still find it astonishing that so many of my friends and professional colleagues seem to know all about New York and Washington and San Francisco—even Los Angeles and Houston—but have never been to Chicago, one of the world's great cities in all respects.

The Chicago Way of Doing Things

I must admit, however, that to a newcomer, there were some things about Chicago in the 1940s and 1950s that required a little getting used to.

There was a casual attitude toward law and other things governmental—a way to make things work even if it's not entirely by the book. Taxes were something that some Chicagoans took lightly. I learned this after I had been in the Windy City for about a year. I knew there was a state law requiring personal property taxes, but I hadn't paid any, so I went to the Cook County Tax Collector's office, downtown in the Loop, and sought out one of the senior tax collectors. I unburdened myself, confessing that I hadn't paid the tax, and I asked him what I should do. He looked at me in amazement. Then he walked around his desk and put his arm around my shoulder. "Have they caught up with you yet?" he asked. *They?* I thought, *Wasn't he the tax collector?* "No," I said, "*they* haven't." "Well, go on home," he said, "and wait until they catch up with you."

However, that same tax came in handy for me some time later. While I was serving on the Northfield Township Board of Education, we were confronted by an urgent need for new classrooms, to accommodate the first wave of baby boomers. But we didn't have the money. Someone suggested collecting the personal property tax. We talked to Mr. Seul, the township treasurer. He was skeptical, because it had never been collected. But we suggested that we simply bill everybody $25 a family. They would hardly notice it, they would pay it, and we would have the money for the classrooms. He did, they did, and we go the classrooms built.

Another example: After I had been sweet-talked into serving as treasurer of the Chicago Press Club, I discovered that we hadn't been paying the federal dues tax. We were delinquent by nearly $75,000. I discussed our predicament with Bob Hurleigh, news director of *Chicago Tribune*'s radio and TV stations, WGN. We had 150 members, but if we reported that many we'd have to pay up the whole delinquency. We didn't have the money, and we would have to close the club. "Let's go talk to Pete Green (recently past Gov. Dwight H. Green, then practicing law on LaSalle Street)," Bob said. "Maybe he'll represent us *pro bono*."

So we went to see former Governor Green, and it turned out that he had an even better idea. He suggested that we pretend that the club had just been revived and had only 25 members. We could afford to pay the dues tax for that many. Then each year thereafter, we'd report a few more members and pay a little more tax. In three or four years, we would be straight with the law. The government would get its money, we would still be alive, and everything would be copasetic. It wasn't exactly legal, but it worked. (Green had made his reputation in the 1930s prosecuting big-time tax evaders in Chicago, most notably gangster Al Capone, so he probably thought our non-compliance was pretty minor.)

Perhaps the most vivid example of the Chicago spirit of "living with things as they are" came from a Chicago police officer who was assigned to reducing gang violence. I met him while I was serving as chairman of Mayor Richard J. Daley's Chicago Youth Commission in 1956. We were talking about the bloody battles between street gangs on the South Side, the West Side and the North Side—all around the town. Different nationalities, different races, different religions, all bent on doing each other in.

"What do you tell them?" I asked the officer. "I tell them they don't have to *love* their neighbor, they don't have to *like* their neighbor. They can *hate* their neighbor, as far as I'm concerned. They just can't *kill* their neighbor." There it is, the Chicago way. Look at things they way they are and figure out a way to make it all work.

10

TV, or Not TV

By the end of 1950 I'd been writing the "The Round Table" column in the *Chicago Journal of Commerce* for about two years. I was on vacation in Maine with Gogo when I received a telephone call from my friend Gerry Schnur, a financial public relations man who had a number of influential clients in Chicago. "Kip, have you ever thought of television?" he asked me. "Yes," I said, "I've been thinking about buying a set, but the boys are still young, so we haven't gotten around to it yet."

"No," said Gerry, "I'm talking about you going on television with a news program." I thought that was ridiculous, and I told him so. "I'm a writer, not a broadcaster. I'm a print reporter. I do columns and all that sort of thing, and I write about business."

But Gerry kept on talking. "My client is Lester Armour—*the* Armour, of meat packing fame. He is chairman of the Chicago National Bank, and he wants to sponsor a program of general news and business news, hosted by someone who could cover business without insulting their directors and business clients." I promised to give it some thought. In my work at the *Journal of*

Commerce, I had made a few talks around the city, but I hadn't done any broadcasting.

Eventually, I decided to give it a try. Gerry arranged an appointment with Mr. Armour in his boardroom at the bank, on LaSalle Street at the corner of Monroe. We came to an agreement, and shortly thereafter I began doing the program every evening at 6 p.m. over WGN-TV. Though this was the *Chicago Tribune* station (whose call letters reflected the paper's boastful slogan, "World's Great Newspaper"), my program was independent. I would leave my office at the *Journal of Commerce* on West Grand Avenue, walk two blocks to the Chicago Tribune Tower, take the elevator up to the WGN studios, and start reading the news wires. After two hours of work—digesting the day's events and writing ten minutes of news copy to deliver on the air—I was ready...and almost perpetually terrified. I would be talking to tens of thousands, maybe hundreds of thousands, of viewers throughout the Middle West. WGN-TV, as the "Voice of *The Chicago Tribune*," had an enormous audience, and even though I was not a member of "the WGN team," I would be broadcasting to all those people.

The manager of WGN-TV and radio, Bob Hurleigh, would provide me with a desk and access to the wires. I would have designated studio facilities, a camera crew, director, stage hands and other paraphernalia, but beyond that, I was on my own, to decide on content, produce the script, invite interview guests, set things up and bring it off. It was daunting, but so was everything in television in those days. No one had any experience (although the radio journalists had a head-start on us print guys). It was all catch-as-catch-can.

For me this experience had another unexpected consequence: It doubled my pay overnight. The television news program paid me as much money as I was receiving as a columnist for the *Journal of Commerce*. Never before had I received a doubling of income instantaneously. (In San Francisco as a cub reporter, I had received a 50% raise, from $16 a week to $24 a week.) Life was coming up roses.

Learning TV Journalism

On the air, at 6 o'clock in the evening, I usually led off with the Korean War, which had begun in June of 1950, and the progress of American forces in combat. I had learned to spell the Korean place names, but now I had to pronounce them too. I decided to be authentic, so I got in touch with a professor of Asian languages at the University of Chicago to find out the correct sounds of that arcane language. I quickly discovered that the audience (and even my TV crew) didn't know what I was talking about. So I went back to calling Pyongyang "pee-ong-yang" with a good Midwestern twang.

In the start-up days of television, visuals had to be produced *ex tempore* and in house. War maps that came over the wires could be reproduced in newspapers but were not useful for television—the scale was not right. Television required motion, and the photos of battle scenes were stills, so we had to create our own motion. In cooperation with the director in the control room, I would move a wooden pointer across a map of the battle scene. Simultaneously, the cameraman would pan his studio camera across the still photo propped up on an easel. Together we would create the impression of motion. It was an early case of television trying to pretend that we—and you—were there.

Later that year, a band of Puerto Rican nationalists shocked Washington and the country by attacking members of Congress at the Capitol and trying to shoot President Truman, who was then staying at Blair House during reconstruction of the White House across the street. The attacks had come so unexpectedly that we were receiving no photos. The TV director asked me to describe the scene, since I knew the layout of streets and buildings around the White House. I drew a primitive map and gave it to the staff artist. By airtime we had an accurate depiction of the scene, across Pennsylvania Avenue from the White House, complete with positions of the guards, angles of attack and the line of fire.

At Christmas time, the new medium of television was anxious to display the family side of the news staff, so I invited Gogo to bring our two sons, Todd and Knight, into the studio for the program on Christmas day. She ushered in the boys, aged five and almost three, and at the appointed moment, Knight sat on the stool and told the audience about Santa's visit. But five-year-old Todd mischievously grabbed the map pointer and roared around the studio shouting, "In Korea today....," while everyone in the studio tried to catch him by the arm. The cameras switched away as we caught the rampant "reporter," and we all sighed with relief.

Going National on Radio

One day in 1951 I got a call from the news director of the ABC radio network, Bill Ray, asking if I would be interested in doing a

10 o'clock national news program. He said the respected, gravelly voiced ABC news commentator Elmer Davis was ailing and thinking about relinquishing his 10 o'clock spot. He said I could take on this assignment in addition to my 6 p.m. local new show on WGN-TV, but I knew that I probably couldn't manage to also continue writing my daily column at the *Journal of Commerce*. By coincidence, changes were being made at my paper. *The Wall Street Journal* had recently bought it from the Ridder family, and it looked as though my front-page column would no longer be needed. (Before long the venerable Chicago business paper was transformed into the Midwest edition of *The Wall Street Journal*.)

So I accepted the ABC offer and went on national radio. Sen. Joseph McCarthy was on a rampage against communist spies in the federal government—a real and dangerous situation in Washington since the late 1940s, but one that was being wildly overblown by the demagogic GOP senator from Wisconsin. Elmer Davis had been one of the nation's leading crusaders against McCarthy's irresponsible charges. Every night he had treated his audience to a hard-charging attack, lambasting McCarthy from stem to stern. It roused the listeners but left little time for general news.

While the Elmer Davis formula clearly appealed to many in his audience, I thought McCarthy had actually benefited from the broadcaster's attacks. In my opinion, McCarthy needed to be downgraded and put "on page 5," as it were, rather than page 1. I led my broadcasts with more important topics: the Marshall Plan for Europe, the economy, foreign aid, civil rights, the Korean War and President Truman's differences with Gen. Douglas MacArthur over the conduct of it. In my daily news coverage, I treated the

McCarthy charges coolly and skeptically, as the senator's trumped-up allegations became increasingly transparent. During one of his visits to Chicago, I met him with a group of reporters and asked for some evidence to back up his latest charges. With a very studied gesture, he reached down to pat his briefcase and said, "It's all right here." But he never opened his briefcase and never offered any proof.

During the height of the furor, I was invited to address a business audience in northern Wisconsin, an area that was clearly McCarthy territory. When it came time for me to speak, I made a "battlefield decision." I would talk about important national and world issues without mentioning the inflammatory political subject of McCarthyism. When I opened the floor to questions, I was asked about the Cold War, the economy, communist influence in the United States, and related subjects. Then I was approached by a man who appeared to be on the verge of apoplexy. He pointed his finger at me and shouted, "You just insulted the greatest living American." I tried to think who that could be: Dwight Eisenhower? Chief Justice Warren? Charles A. Lindbergh? "Who do you mean?" I asked. And he shouted back, "Senator Joseph McCarthy!" I responded in puzzlement, "But I didn't mention him." "That's just it!" he said angrily, and stalked off.

The Elmer Davis radio audience was addicted to a steady diet of tirades against Joe McCarthy. They didn't take at all well to my calm and balanced approach, and they told ABC in no uncertain terms in their calls and letters. The network brass and I had a talk, with the result that I got my own news show at 11 o'clock, and the

10 o'clock show was turned over to Quincy Howe, a well-known liberal journalist. The switch received plaudits from both audiences.

Interviewing Famous Figures

When significant national figures visited Chicago, I would bring them onto my evening program for interviews. On one occasion my guest was financier Joseph P. Kennedy, the first chairman of the Securities and Exchange Commission, former ambassador to Great Britain, and father of the junior senator from Massachusetts, John F. Kennedy, who in 1956 would be talked about as a possible vice president on the Democratic ticket. Kennedy the father had long been an isolationist, which I was not (nor was his son), but the interview was popular with the Midwestern isolationists in my radio audience. When the program ended, we exchanged thoughts and observations on Washington, *The Kiplinger Washington Letter* (which he read), and what his son and I were doing in our professions. Later he wrote to my father in Washington, and the two men exchanged correspondence about the rising careers of their sons.

Some time later I received a call from a man identifying himself as "Sergeant Shriver." As I was doing a series on the military at nearby Ft. Sheridan, I assumed this was a public affairs man from the base, so I said, "Certainly, sergeant, what can I do for you?" It turned out not to be an officer from Ft. Sheridan, but *Sargent* Shriver, a son-in-law of Joseph P. Kennedy and manager of the Chicago Merchandise Mart, the enormous office edifice that was owned by the Kennedy family. What he wanted was to invite Gogo and me to dinner with him and his wife, Eunice Kennedy Shriver.

Asserting Professional Standards

In the 1950s, TV newsrooms were inhabited by print and radio reporters who were being reprogrammed into television journalists. We had our professional organization called ARTNA, the Association of Radio and Television News Analysts. In addition to the customary professional concerns, we were deeply involved with the principle of editorial independence. We sought insulation from the commercialization that was creeping into the whole broadcast industry, news included. (Sponsors had long been prominent inside radio entertainment and even news programming, getting their names on shows and product plugs inside drama and comedies.) We TV newsmen were generally okay with the sponsors' names appearing on camera, on the news studio set, and Admiral (the popular maker of TV sets) had it's logo behind the desk where I delivered the news. But we reporters and commentators were continually pressured by sponsors to voice the ads that accompanied our broadcasts, and we tried to draw a line against that.

Among the sponsors of my local TV show was McLaughlin's Manor House Coffee, whose owner lived in Lake Forest, not far from where I lived in Northfield. After I had been doing the news program for some months, Mr. McLaughlin invited me to have lunch with him. "If you would do the commercials," he told me, "they would have much more impact, and you could make more money." We chatted amicably, but finally I worked up the courage to say to him that I was a newsman, not a commercial announcer, and my endorsement of his product would call into question my objectivity as a news reporter. "If my opinions were for sale to any sponsor," I asked, "how much value would my judgment have as a news analyst?"

Mr. McLaughlin didn't get the point. Then an idea occurred to me. I knew that he was an admirer of Walter Lippmann, the venerated political columnist of *The New York Times*. So I said to Mr. McLauglin, "Would you require Walter Lippmann to voice your commercials on the air?" "Oh, no," he said, "that would not be appropriate." I responded, "Well, then, don't ask me to." I continued to do the program without doing the commercials.

A Show Called *Impact*

More than a decade before the "TV news magazine" concept became popular in the 1960s (first in Canada and then on CBS's *60 Minutes* in the U.S.), Chicago viewers were treated every week to an innovative show called *Impact*. It was a live, unedited half-hour of interviews, human-interest features, breaking news, scenes behind the scenes, and situation reports, with all the malaprops and mix-ups of real, live, on-the-spot television. And in the audience ratings of those days, it got the largest viewing audience of any non-sports, non-entertainment program in Chicago. It was a fast-paced, slam-bang program, and I was its host.

How it came to pass, as with all things television in those years, was somewhat accidental. I had been doing the evening television news and radio commentary for ABC, with offices in the Chicago Daily News Building, across the river from ABC's studios in the Opera Building on Wacker Drive. Downstairs at the *Chicago Daily*

News, Jack Mabley was writing a column about television. At heart, however, he was still a general newsman. (Jack would eventually become the star local columnist of the *Chicago Tribune*, writing 8,000 columns on a wide range of issues.) One day I got a call from Jack, asking if we at ABC would be interested in collaborating with *The Daily News* on a new kind of TV program. I talked it over with Con O'Day, the ABC affiliate's news director, and he agreed that it would be worth pursuing.

Out of these conversations came *Impact*, which aired on Thursday evenings, using *Daily News* reporters and editors on breaking stories. I was the host, interviewer and on-air "personality." Mabley and I worked together on the schedule and content, and we jointly lined up interviews. The format was flexible—no fixed pattern or rules, except to be newsworthy and interesting.

Our programs originated live from inside the studio and from remote locations— places like Skid Row, where I interviewed derelict alcoholics ("winos," they were called back then), captured by our cameraman through the window of our truck along West Madison Street. We took an inside look at Chicago's firehouse in the Loop, where our equipment blew an electrical circuit, plunging the firehouse into darkness (but leaving our audio intact). We telecast from an ore boat tied up at South Chicago, a dance at the Cook County Hospital mental ward, and blast furnaces at U.S. Steel's Chicago mill. We visited the electric chair in the execution chamber at Cook County Jail. We toured the Chicago railroad yards west of the Loop. I interviewed a street prostitute and drug addict, who managed to clean up her language for the broadcast but concealed her identity with a black bag over her head. We walked our TV viewers through the interior of German submarine U-505, which was moored as a museum on the Lake Michigan shoreline in downtown Chicago, and did an interview with Admiral Dan Gallery, who as a Navy captain in 1944 had led the capture of the sub in the Atlantic Ocean.

One of the most memorable of our *Impact* programs was a visit with Dr. Enrico Fermi, the University of Chicago physicist and "Father of the Atomic Age," on the 10th anniversary of the world's first "self-sustaining nuclear reaction," which took place in Chicago in 1942, unbeknownst to the world. It was this super-secret experiment that led three years later to the dropping of the atomic bombs on Hiroshima and Nagasaki, bringing the surrender of Japan and the end of World War II.

The reaction was engineered in a laboratory fashioned from a concrete squash court under the massive stands of Stagg Field, the university's football stadium. Fermi's team had produced an energy source that had never been known to mankind, a secret of nature as powerful as fire. It was more than Prometheus could have imagined.

I asked Dr. Fermi if we could bring a crew of television people, with cameras, to talk to him and film the scene where this had taken place. But before we brought that whole outfit, I had lunch with him at the university's faculty club on its South Side campus. There I saw two Enrico Fermis. At lunch, the Italian immigrant physicist talked in warm, almost grandfatherly tones, like an old-country patriarch. When faculty members came over to pay their respects to the Nobel laureate, his tone was collegial and gentle. But later, during our interview in the laboratory, the other Dr. Fermi emerged:

the sharp, incisive, intellectual, unemotional scientist at work. He unfolded the story as I had never heard it before. And I am sure that hundreds of thousands of Chicago television viewers had the same experience.

Impact also aired a program highlighting another group of Italian-Americans—the Mafia. In Washington the Kefauver Committee was investigating the undercover operations of the Chicago "Mob." In Prohibition days, the mob handled illegal sales of liquor, with Al Capone as top boss. Chicago secretly prided itself on being the site of the St. Valentine's Day Massacre—a bloody reprisal by one gang against another. Now "the Mob" was "the Mafia"—the same characters with a different name. Chicago reporters were continually chronicling their movements. With Con O'Day, I decided that I ought to take the *Impact* cameras to River Forest, the upscale western suburb of Chicago that was favored by top Mafia bosses, to visit the homes of Tony ("Big Tuna") Accardo, Sam ("Moon") Giancana, and Paul ("The Waiter") Ricca. My wife was apprehensive about the plan, but I assured her that, as long as the cameras were on me, I would be all right.

On the appointed day, we drove first to the home of Sam Giancana, who was known as the enforcer of Mafia orders—a trigger man, the superintendent of assassination. Giancana lived in a modest, single-level house on the less-elegant side of River Forest, and we approached his house and rang the doorbell. Nobody answered. I waited and decided that, of course, he had been tipped off and was not about to show up. So we left, but not before I noticed that all the windows had metal grates securely attached—to prevent anyone from lobbing a Molotov cocktail at the glass.

Next stop was the home of Paul Ricca, who had been convicted of racketeering and was on parole, meaning that he was not allowed to leave his residence without court permission. So, we figured, he had to be there, and he would benefit from being seen. Sure enough, he answered the doorbell, came out onto the porch and greeted me in a warm, effusive manner. I couldn't have asked for a more pleasant reception—except that he wouldn't answer any of my questions, because his lawyer told him not to.

Now on to Tony Accardo—the "Big Tuna," the biggest of the bosses. His home occupied a whole city block, surrounded by gardens. It was the former home of the president of the Majestic Radio Corporation, one of the largest manufacturers of home radio sets in the days before television. I walked up the front path and noticed, on both sides of the entrance, two burly "gardeners" in khaki overalls, who looked as though they were bulging with armaments underneath. They watched me like hawks, but I proceeded to the door and rang the bell. It was answered by a maid. I asked if I could speak with Mr. Accardo. "He's not home," she said. I asked if I might speak with Mrs. Accardo. "She's not home." I explained that I was from the ABC television station, WBKB, and I would like to ask for a statement. The door was slammed shut. The two "gardeners" closed in from behind. I turned slowly and executed that old Navy aviation maneuver called "getting the hell out of there."

To Chicago audiences in the early 1950s, these *Impact* programs were breathtaking. They became topics of conversation at work and on the trains and buses that carried Chicagoans everywhere. Day after day, I would be accosted—on State Street or Michigan Avenue—by enthusiastic viewers who called out and waved and shouted greetings from passing cars. The excitement garnered by television in its early years was like the attention that pop music stars would get from their teenaged audiences later in the 1950s and '60s.

To me, the professional stimulation of my work outweighed my new celebrity. Yes, I was a recognized face around Chicago, and my wife and I would be photographed having dinner at popular restaurants. But it meant more to me to be named by *TV Guide* as the outstanding TV newsman in Chicago in 1953, and profiled in *Newsweek* magazine as "The Cool Young Voice" in 1955.

Trying to Take *Impact* National

I had hopes that ABC would pick up our local hit, *Impact*, and replicate its formula in other cities. There was plenty of precedent for this, because Chicago was a strong "Second City" to the center of the broadcast universe, New York—and, in many ways, more innovative than New York. Since the dawn of commercial television in the late 1940s, Chicago had been the spawning ground of an unusual number of talented broadcast journalists, producers and local programs that were later picked up by national networks.

For example, Dave Garroway, the first host of NBC's *Today* show in 1952, had pioneered this kind of folksy, conversational program on his own morning show in Chicago. (By coincidence, the first national sponsor of *Today* in '52 was *Changing Times*, the *Kiplinger Magazine*, that my father and I had launched in 1947, and it was the first magazine ever sold on television.)

Seven years before Jim Henson created his Muppets in Washington, D.C. (later made famous on *Sesame Street*), Chicago puppeteer Burr Tillstrom in 1947 created a sophisticated comedy show in Chicago called *Kukla, Fran and Ollie*. On the show, which was popular with kids and adults alike, host Fran Allison (a radio comedienne and singer) chatted with Tillstrom's witty puppets, including Kukla, Oliver J. Dragon (Ollie), Fletcher Rabbit, Beulah Witch and a southern gentleman named Colonel Crackie. Picked up by the NBC network in early '49 and later shown on ABC, *Kukla, Fran and Ollie* was a national hit until 1957.

Another product of Chicago's creative TV community was *Ding Dong School*, a program for young children dubbed "the nursery school of the air." A precursor of the gentle *Mister Rogers*-style of kids' programming, *Ding Dong School* was hosted live by educator Dr. Frances Horwich (called "Miss Frances" on the show), and it ran on the NBC network from 1952 to 1956.

Chicago also produced a number of future network news stars, such as John Chancellor, who was a dogged local reporter for the *Chicago Sun-Times* before working at WMAQ-TV in Chicago and, in 1956, joining NBC network news as a national correspondent (and still later, anchor of the *NBC Nightly News*). The genial Hugh Downs, who had been an announcer on WMAQ in the late '40s (and announcer of *Kukla, Fran and Ollie* in the early '50s), went to New York in 1954 and eventually became host of NBC's *Today* and *20/20* programs.

So, with high hopes for *Impact* going national on ABC, I traveled to New York City to pay a call on John Charles Daly, the network's vice president for news, with whom I had worked during the 1952 Republican and Democratic national conventions. I regaled him with stories of the success of our program and our collaboration with the *Chicago Daily News*. I suggested that a similar program could be produced at ABC stations in New York, Philadelphia, or Boston, in collaboration with one of the leading newspapers in each city.

John listened and then asked, "How much does it cost to produce?" I felt triumphant when I told him that, because of the newspaper affiliation, the cost was surprisingly modest, "around $2,500 a week." John's reaction knocked me dead: "That's too cheap. No sponsor would pay attention to it." I was indignant. "You can charge the sponsor anything you want," I said. "I'm just telling you what it costs."

But the New York mentality won out. It was "too cheap," and ABC passed on it. Twenty years later, when John Daly and I were friends in Washington and went to Redskins football games with team owner Jack Kent Cooke, I needled him about that encounter. I never let him forget it.

11

Politics and Television

Once upon a time, party nominees for president of the United States were selected at great gatherings of people "in convention assembled"—not in the state primaries as they are today. At these great boisterous events, political parties and their factions vied with one another, and committees wrangled over rules. "Favorite sons" waited off stage until their delegations were ready with balloons and streamers and speeches from the podium, and the managers met in hotel rooms to wrangle and deal and exchange promises and finally call for a vote. State delegations huddled on the floor and off, to fashion viable combinations of personalities, promises and policies that would bring success in November. While all this was happening, TV cameras were poking into corners of caucuses, and microphones were picking up off-hand remarks uttered by the unwary.

That was what it was like in the 1950s, a time when deals in smoke-filled rooms were just beginning to give way to more transparent methods of selecting candidates for general elections. A few decades later, the presidential nominee would be decided in a grueling series of state primaries in the spring and early summer, long before the conventions, which would become carefully choreographed showcases for the nominees and their ideas. Today, the only drama left for a convention is the nominee's choice of running mate. But in the early 1950s, the decisions were still being made at conventions and candidates still being selected there, with millions of Americans glued to their television sets at home, waiting to know the final outcome.

The 1948 presidential campaign, Dewey versus Truman, had been the first one to be nationally televised—but only to the small number of homes that had TV sets that year. Coverage consisted largely of "talking heads" sitting at desks reporting results from the conventions and on election night, but with little coverage from the convention floor. The medium had not yet developed the mobility to allow reporters to poke into committee rooms, grab key figures on the floor, and blanket the deliberations, as print reporters had done in the past.

The 1952 Conventions

But after explosive growth in the national television audience over the following four years, the three networks—CBS, NBC and ABC—could afford the staffing and technology to bring the drama of the conventions and election night into America's living rooms. So the 1952 campaign was the first one to be avidly followed by a large portion of the American people. The result was panoramic and up-close coverage of political decision-making that gripped the nation. Night after night, households with new TV sets experienced the head-knocking emotions and behind-the-scenes jockeying that had hitherto only been described after the fact. On their small, flickering, black-and-white TV screens, viewers were looking right over the shoulder of the participants as the choices were being made.

It was my good fortune to be one of the TV reporters who covered the two national conventions of 1952, which (unlike today) were both held in the same city. That city was Chicago, where I anchored the evening news on WBKB-TV, the ABC affiliate, and was therefore asked to be part of the network team ABC assembled to provide its national coverage.

ABC's Team in Chicago

As the smallest and lowest-budget network in that day, ABC had the least resources of camera crews, but our ABC team at the Chicago conventions consisted of top-flight, aggressive radio and TV journalists whose stars would ascend in the following years. There was veteran war correspondent Martin Agronsky, who had participated in ABC's 1948 political coverage and would later host CBS's *Face the Nation* and PBS's *Agronsky & Company.* We had a broadcast newsman from Los Angeles named Chet Huntley, who four years later, would begin co-anchoring NBC's top-rate evening news program. The most experienced member of our team was probably Pauline Frederick, the first woman to achieve prominence in broadcast journalism. She had cut her teeth as an NBC radio correspondent in Europe during World War II and had covered the Nuremberg trials for ABC radio. She would finish her distinguished career back at NBC, where she was longtime chief correspondent at the United Nations.

The 1952 campaign was under way early in the year. President Truman—embattled by an unpopular war in Korea, ethics scandals in his administration and charges of communists in government—was not running for a second full term, so the field was wide open in both parties. For the Republicans, there were several front runners, the most prominent being Sen. Robert Taft from Ohio. But the liberal wing of the party was looking for someone else, and the most frequently mentioned name was Dwight D. Eisenhower—retired general, former commander of Allied forces in Europe in World War II, and later president of Columbia University. He had kept himself free from any political party label, yet many Republicans wanted him to run as a Republican, and the most prominent among his backers was Sen. Henry Cabot Lodge of Massachusetts.

Before the convention began, Senator Lodge came to Chicago, and I went to see him at his hotel, the massive Conrad Hilton on Michigan Avenue. He didn't have much time between appointments, but he agreed to let me ask him questions while he was changing his shirt. I hit the big question head on: "What makes you think General Eisenhower is a Republican?" He stopped, turned around, looked squarely at me, and said very authoritatively: "He *is* a Republican." What he said—and the way he said it— left me convinced that he knew what he was talking about...and he did.

The GOP Goes First

The two national party conventions were both held at the International Amphitheatre in Chicago, and the Republican convention led off in the second week of July. Going into the convention, the totals of likely and probable delegate votes for Eisenhower and Taft were thought to be just about equal. A few southern states, however, hung in the balance, especially Louisiana— an overwhelmingly Democratic state where the Republican Party was largely a phantom organization, springing to life by doling out federal patronage jobs whenever a Republican won the White House, which hadn't happened since 1928.

The newly formed committees for Eisenhower were desperate to get their delegations recognized and seated in order to get their candidate nominated. As the convention progressed, it became increasingly clear that the credentials committee— which would authorize the delegations and give the state's official vote—would determine who the Republican nominee would be.

On the afternoon of the final vote by the credentials committee, I was assigned by ABC-TV to cover the committee deliberations. The meeting was to be held on the fifth floor of the Conrad Hilton. Since NBC and CBS were the senior networks, they had more equipment and more clout. We of ABC had to improvise. With a limited number of camera crews, we were spread thin and frequently had to move to new positions at the last minute. On this occasion, in view of the critical nature of the credentials committee vote, NBC and CBS had sent full crews ahead to position themselves on both sides of the exit door from the committee room. Their correspondents would have an advantage in grabbing the chairman when he announced the decision. We of ABC, I feared, would be relegated to the leftovers— losing the edge of the first report.

The only thing I could think of to counteract their advantage was to use my Chicago reporting experience—my knowledge of the hotel—and find some way to turn it to use. Knowing the corridors and stairwells of the building, I scouted the location of the hearing room, and behind it I found a hall leading to an unused room next to the hearing room. There was a locked door between this room and the hearing room, and I discovered that by lying down with my ear against the gap at the bottom of the door, I could hear everything going on inside.

The debate got heated. The voices rose, and I heard the Eisenhower forces getting more and more vociferous. I figured that when the vote came it would be for Eisenhower. I needed a camera and microphone, so I dashed to the nearest phone, called ABC central and pleaded frantically for a crew. They were incredulous: A camera with pedestal weighed nearly half a ton, and I wanted it pronto on the fifth floor. But the news desk knew the importance of the announcement, so they scrambled to oblige me.

I waited at the front entrance of the committee room, where NBC and CBS had monopolized the door locations, and a few minutes later, the elevator doors opened and out came the ABC crew—camera, microphone, cables and all. I muscled into position in front of the other two networks, while my crew untangled the cables and dropped them down the elevator shaft. Suddenly the committee room doors were flung open. Before anyone had time to ask for a statement, I grabbed the chairman and confronted him with the fact that I already knew the vote. He acknowledged the facts, and the ABC-TV audience got the first word that Eisenhower would likely be the Republican candidate.

A Panel of Pundits

Midway through the '52 Republican convention there was a lull. The ABC news desk decided to air a panel of its "experts" to keep its ratings up. Each reporter or commentator on the panel would be expected to make the case for one of the big-name potential candidates, and it would be an audience attention-getter. The prospective nominees were, besides Senator Taft and General Eisenhower, former Minnesota Gov. Harold Stassen and Gen. Douglas MacArthur, who had now become the nemesis of President Harry Truman, who had removed him from command in Korea.

For added journalistic strength in its coverage, ABC had formed a working alliance with *Newsweek* magazine, so on Wednesday night the combined forces of ABC and *Newsweek* were put together for the high-level panel discussion. The panelists included Agronsky, Huntley, and Ernest Lindley of *Newsweek*, an experienced Washington political journalist whom I had worked with ten years earlier on my father's book about Washington. At 33 years old, I was the junior member of the panel in age and broadcast experience—well-known in Chicago news but a newcomer on the national television scene.

The half-hour discussion took up the possible nominees, one by one. The panelists pontificated on the candidate's strengths and weaknesses, showing respect for each man's chances of being the nominee. When it finally came to Gen. Douglas MacArthur, the discussion morphed into an almost hushed, reverential tone. Here was a national hero, a man of brilliance. Here was a man of extraordinary experience in administration—witness his performance as the virtual emperor of Japan during the American occupation. Here was a serious and viable candidate for President of the United States.

"Now wait a minute," came a hesitant voice down at the end of the table. It was my voice. I was only a young, regional newsman in Chicago, but I didn't think the general was a serious possibility as a candidate for President—and I said so. Brilliant he was, I said, but he'd never been a politician. His entire life had been lived in the military. He had never run for elective office. He had never had to deal with conflicting national political factions. He had never taken guff from congressional committees. And he was 74 years old. In short, I said, this brilliant American is not a viable candidate for President on either ticket.

There was a stunned silence, and I was struck with apprehension about what I had said. It was what most objective political reporters thought, but I had broken ranks with my senior colleagues, and I had the sinking feeling that I would be in trouble tomorrow—maybe even fired.

The next day dawned—no repercussions, a day of steady work. It was Thursday, and the candidate would soon be chosen. Toward evening, as the news staff was drinking coffee in the ABC newsroom, in walked Robert Kintner, then president of the network, a wise political commentator in his own right who had co-authored (with the influential Washington pundit Joseph Alsop) an authoritative, nationally syndicated column on politics. When I was introduced to him, his face brightened up, and without any warning, he drew me aside and said, *sotto voce*, "I just want to tell you, your comments on the panel last night were the best I heard." (I didn't get fired.)

The Democrats Come to Chicago

After the GOP nominated Eisenhower and his running mate—the young senator from California, Richard M. Nixon—the Democrats met a few weeks later in the same Chicago venue. The field of Democratic challengers for the nomination in 1952 was particularly crowded. Front-runners included senators Estes Kefauver of Tennessee and Richard Russell of Georgia, former Commerce Secretary and U.S. Ambassador Averell Harriman, and the current Vice President, Alben W. Barkley, a former senator from Kentucky. There was a lot of talk about Illinois Gov. Adlai Stevenson, who protested that he was not a candidate. But his stirring opening speech at the convention, in his own hometown, stimulated his supporters' efforts to draft him as the nominee.

Vice President Barkley desperately wanted the top spot, but most people thought he was too old at 78. Members of the press corps agreed, and apparently most of the convention delegates did too. Midway through convention week, the Vice President's office called to set up a press conference, and I was assigned to cover it for ABC-TV. It was at Barkley headquarters in the Blackstone Hotel.

When I arrived at his suite, I looked around for a telephone and found one—the only phone in the place. I commandeered it, and the only way I could hold it was to call ABC in New York, long distance, and tell them to stay on the line. The wait seemed interminable, but I kept the line open. After more than half an hour, Barkley appeared, and, as we expected, sadly announced that he was withdrawing from the race. I shouted into the phone, "OK, he said it! Put it on the air!" ABC broke the news before the other networks. Then the hotel operator came on the line and asked me who to charge the call to. I told her to put it on the ABC bill. "I can't do that; they're not registered in the hotel," she said. "Well, who's paying for this room?" I asked. "That's the Vice President's suite," she said. I told her to put it on the Vice President's bill, and she did. I hoped he would forgive me.

After Barkley's withdrawal, the convention proceeded to balloting. Stevenson was showing signs of accepting a draft, but Kefauver led him, Russell and Harriman through the first two ballots. On the third ballot, Harriman withdrew, and a host of "favorite-son" candidates threw their delegates to Stevenson, leading to his eventual nomination. A southern conservative, Sen. John Sparkman of Alabama, was picked as his running mate, to try to balance the Illinois governor's northern liberalism.

On the July night that Adlai Stevenson received the Democratic nomination, a news conference was scheduled at the home of a friend, Chicago investment banker William McCormick Blair, in an up-scale neighborhood along North State Street. The event would be held inside the walled garden of the home, and it would be limited to a small pool of reporters. When the names were announced, there was no one from ABC, but Pauline Frederick and I decided that one of us would try to get in. As the reporters filed into the house, Pauline and I concluded that one of us would have to go over the wall. She had started her broadcast career in 1939 as NBC radio's director of women's programming, and while she quickly outgrew that assignment and went into international news, she had always struggled not to be typecast as a "women's reporter." But the wall was eight feet tall, and Pauline was wearing a skirt, so the assignment fell to me. With a boost from a friend, I pulled up, clawed my way over the top, and dropped down inside the garden. As it turned out, the candidate didn't say anything newsworthy, but at least we could report that "ABC was there."

With NBC in 1956

The drama of the 1952 conventions in Chicago, shown live in America's living rooms, cemented the role of television news as a rapidly growing force in American politics. It also led to career changes for a number of us on the ABC convention team. Several—Frederick, Huntley, and Agronsky—joined our well-heeled rival, NBC News, as network correspondents based in various cities. I remained in Chicago television news, but I moved in 1955 from ABC's affiliate, WBKB, to NBC's Chicago station, WMAQ. Robert Kintner, who was credited with raising the stature of ABC in its competition with CBS and NBC (with such bold initiatives as broadcasting the entire, riveting Army-McCarthy hearings live), later decamped for NBC, too, becoming its president in 1958.

In the political summer of 1956, the Republicans had the simple task of renominating the popular ticket of Eisenhower and Nixon, which they did by acclamation in San Francisco that August. The Democrats returned to their convention site of four years before, Chicago, so once again I was part of a network coverage team, but this time for NBC.

Adlai Stevenson beat back a challenge from Averell Harriman and was easily nominated on the first ballot. But Stevenson had a surprise for the delegates. He told them that—for the first time ever—*they*, not the presidential nominee or bosses in a smoke-filled room, would pick the vice presidential nominee in open balloting on the convention floor. Heightening the excitement was the fact that contenders for the running-mate slot had only one day to gather the support of delegates.

Among the more than a dozen vice-presidential hopefuls were both Tennessee senators, Estes Kefauver and Albert Gore, Sr., Massachusetts Sen. John F. Kennedy, New York Mayor Robert Wagner, Jr., Minnesota Sen. Hubert Humphrey, and North Carolina Gov. Luther Hodges. There was also some talk about the powerful Sen. Robert S. Kerr of Oklahoma, a former governor and rich oil man (founder of Kerr-McGee Oil) who had been a presidential hopeful four years before. I found Kerr at the convention and asked if he would be satisfied with the second spot on the ticket. He asked me, "Have you got it to offer?" and I replied, "No." And he replied, "Well, I'll answer that when you do."

A surprisingly strong contender for the V.P. nomination in 1956 was John Kennedy, who was relatively unknown without much of a record in his first term in the Senate. But he got a big push from his wealthy and ambitious father, who was promoting him as a comer in national politics. Kennedy led the balloting after the second round and was within a few votes of getting on the ticket. Then several favorite-son hopefuls threw their delegates to Kefauver, and Kennedy made a magnanimous concession speech. Historians note that Kennedy won points that day for a good fight and a graceful exit—and he also spared himself being on a ticket that was trounced in a landslide by the Republicans that fall. Four years later, he took the top prize as the Democratic standard bearer and went on to the White House.

Career Choices

The most notable winning team to emerge from the 1956 Democratic convention in Chicago were not politicians, but two broadcast journalists—NBC's Washington-based newsman David Brinkley and my former ABC teammate, Chet Huntley. They won plaudits for their co-anchoring of NBC's convention coverage, and that fall, they were teamed together to share the Huntley-Brinkley evening news program.

In light of my success in Chicago, I was beginning to get feelers from NBC in New York about the possibility of my moving there to become part of a national news team. I gave it some thought. To be on any of these teams would be a definite path to the top in the TV news world.

But there were other considerations. My father, then 65 years old, told me that he needed some help at the office. He was overseeing both *The Kiplinger Washington Letter* and *Changing Times* magazine, as well as watching the business side of the company too, and he felt he needed a hand. I had worked on the *Letter* and had helped to start the magazine. I shared the family name with the publications. The work was something I had loved. So when my father broached the subject of my returning to Washington in a senior editorial and executive position, I took it seriously. It had been eight years since I had left my father's business, and when he asked me to return, I said yes.

I had loved my work in television and had learned to live with its pressures. I worked nights, sometimes doing both the 6 o'clock and 11 o'clock news programs. I was never home on weeknights with the family. I slept late and wasn't up when the boys left for school. Staying in television would mean more of such a limited family life.

I made a fast trip to Washington to seal the deal with my father. I bought a house in Chevy Chase, and by September of 1956, Gogo and I and the boys had moved in. The kids were enrolled at North Chevy Chase Elementary, and I was back at The Kiplinger Washington Editors.

When friends asked if I missed television—the helter-skelter pace, the glamour, the thrill of being on top of breaking news as it happened—I told them I was so busy with my new duties in Washington that I hadn't had time to miss it.

12

Getting a Handle on Washington

Sometimes you understand a place better after you have been away from it for a while. When I came back to Washington in 1956, it struck me again how different Washington was from other American cities. While I had grown up around Washington, I had launched my professional news career in San Francisco and Chicago, which both had distinctive hometown atmospheres, personalities and traditions. Like most big American cities, each had an intrinsic sense of place, with a civic structure and an "establishment" of movers and shakers who could get things done almost as a matter of course.

For eight years I had observed this first-hand in Chicago, but now back in Washington, I found it missing in the Nation's Capital—an "artificial" city whose primary business was government. Its business leaders, by and large, headed much smaller enterprises than Chicago's, and they didn't seem to have the clout to get things done.

A case in point: At about the same time, in the early 1950s, local interests in most large cities, including Washington and Chicago, decided—independently of each other—to create public broadcasting stations as part of the new educational television movement. It was all made possible by the 1952 decision of the Federal Communications Commission (FCC) to broaden the broadcast spectrum and make bandwidth available to nonprofit community TV stations (and new-fangled FM radio stations, too). Civic leaders in Chicago decreed in 1953 that that an educational television station be created there, and it *was* created. Its first broadcast was in the fall of 1955.

But in Washington, the local effort was struggling. My father was a prime mover in the original group of incorporators for the Greater Washington Educational Television Association (GWETA) in 1953, but they were having a hard time generating interest and funding among the capital's business and civic leaders.

He phoned me one day in Chicago and asked, "What goes on out there? How did Chicago get it going so fast?" So I told him, and it went something like this: Edward L. Ryerson, chairman of Inland Steel, decided that Chicago ought to have an educational television station. He probably called his friends who were CEOs of other large Chicago-based corporations, such as International Harvester, Sears Roebuck, Montgomery Ward, and the big banks, such as First National, City National, Continental Illinois, and Northern Trust. He probably invited them to lunch together at the Chicago Club. (They would know that Col. Robert McCormick of the *Chicago Tribune* wouldn't come, but he would send somebody and end up supporting the project.) Over lunch they would agree to start a public TV station. They would go back after lunch, assign people in their offices to do the work, and decide on funding commitments. Two years later, WTTW-11 would be on the air in Chicago, in the fall of 1955.

In Washington it took *eight* years. People joined and left the board, and there were constant money problems. Washington in the 1950s was a much smaller metro area than it is today, with no corporations the size of Chicago's. W. M. Kiplinger was the early leader of the effort and remained the public face of the project, but in 1957 he convinced Elizabeth Campbell, a fellow board member and energetic local educator, to take on the presidency and operational responsibility. But by 1960, funds were still so tight that my father sometimes covered WETA's staff payroll out of his personal checkbook, while making space available in the basement of our office building on H Street, N.W for the WETA staff. He went begging to the Ford Foundation in New York for a grant. Finally, in the fall of 1961, WETA made its inaugural broadcast.

Here was a clear demonstration of the differences between Chicago—"a real American city"—and Washington, a national and world capital. Not that there aren't powerful people in Washington—a lot of them—but the fate of the city of Washington is not their central interest.

Movers and Shakers

I saw this again in 1964, when the Rev. Paul Moore arrived for his new assignment as suffragan bishop (second in command) of the Episcopal diocese of Washington, based at the Washington Cathedral. Filled with fervor and determined to do good in his new community, he cast around for guidance and advice. I met him as the result of a telephone call from my friend and Maryland neighbor Newbold Noyes, Jr., editor of *The Evening Star*, Washington's afternoon daily.

"Kip," he said, "come to dinner at my house and meet my old friend, Paul Moore. We went to school together at St. Paul's and Yale, and I want to help him get acquainted in Washington."

So Gogo and I had dinner with Bishop Moore at Newbie and Beppie Noyes' home in Potomac, and after dinner we all talked. The minister wanted his church to be not only a place for Sunday worship but also a force for social justice in the Washington community. He wanted to know "how to get a handle on Washington," how he could assemble the core of the community—"that handful of people" who form the central cadre, those movers and shakers who could decide what to do and then get it done.

I told him, "It doesn't happen that way in Washington. There is no inner circle. There is no single axis around which everything revolves. There is no such thing in Washington." But Bishop Moore was adamant. He had just spent seven years in Indianapolis, and he knew other cities too. Every one of them had a core group which could make things move. I repeated my point: Washington is many cities, a combination of many circles. Sometimes they intersect, like the rings of the old Ballentine Beer logo, but never totally coincide.

Democrats and Republicans speak together but meet separately, I told him. The House and Senate move in their own orbits. Judges and lawyers tend to flock together. Executives of national corporations and large local businesses—members of the Federal City Council, all hard-working, dedicated people—undertake great projects, but they operate by committee. The President? He's the biggest man in town, but he doesn't control traffic on the 14th Street Bridge. The Vice President? Important in national councils, but he doesn't affect local zoning or attract economic development. The Dean of the Diplomatic Corps? He is an important personage, but he is no help in affecting the fluid discharge from the Blue Plains Sewage Treatment Plant. In higher education, the dozen institutions of the Consortium of Colleges and Universities seldom act in concert. The World Bank controls billions of dollars worth of social, economic and humanitarian work around the world, but in local Washington, its greatest impact is as the target of anti-globalization protests and extra work for the local police.

Special Interests and Causes

Yet despite all this, everyone seems to want some influence in Washington—the Washington that represents the country at large, the Washington that seems to be everybody's stomping ground. Washington becomes the focus of more cause organizations than any other single place in the world. Since Americans are great joiners, nearly everyone belongs to something that has an office in the Nation's Capital. These offices are headquarters of groups with a point of view. They may be charities, social movements, trade associations, labor movements, endowments, think tanks, or societies for the improvement of...pick your own cause. If they represent something we believe in, they are a part of the democratic process. If not, they are "special interests."

That's the way it is in Washington. Everyone has an ax to grind—good, bad or indifferent—and everyone has someone to help them grind it. But the city itself—hometown Washington—is an anomaly, something everyone thinks he understands but really never does.

Washington, D.C. is not really a "city." It is a federal district, 69 square miles surrounded by Maryland and Virginia. Its citizens don't have voting rights in Congress. It doesn't have a senator. It has a "sort of" member of the House of Representatives, but she has no vote on the floor. (But its citizens *can* vote for President and Vice President of the United States.)

Business corporations want their voice heard in Washington, but they prefer not to have their names mentioned in that connection. They want to be known as being from somewhere else—Pittsburgh, Dallas, Chicago, New York, Los Angeles, or Omaha.

So, the plain truth is, if you want to "get a handle on Washington," be from somewhere else, but be sure to come now and then to enjoy the view.